WORSHIP IN SPIRIT AND TRUTH

Colin Dye

Sovereign World

Sovereign World Ltd
PO Box 777
Tonbridge
Kent TN11 0ZS
England

Scriptural quotations are from the New King James Version, Thomas Nelson Inc., 1991.

ISBN 1 85240 214 8

Typeset by CRB Associates, Reepham, Norfolk
Printed in England by Redwood Books Ltd

FOREWORD

The material in this *Sword of the Spirit* series has been developed over the past ten years at Kensington Temple in London as we have sought to train leaders for the hundreds of churches and groups we have established. Much of the material was initially prepared for the students who attend the International Bible Institute of London – which is based at our church.

Over the years, other churches and colleges have asked if they may use some of our material to help them establish training courses for leaders in their towns and countries. This series has been put together partly to meet this growing need, as churches everywhere seek to train large numbers of new leaders to serve the growth that God is giving.

The material has been constantly refined – by myself, by the students as they have responded, by my many associate pastors, and by the staff at the Bible Institute. In particular, my colleague Timothy Pain has been responsible for sharpening, developing and shaping my different courses and notes into this coherent series.

I hope that many people will use this series in association with our developing Satellite Bible School, but I also pray that churches around the world will use the books to train leaders.

We live at a time when increasing numbers of new churches are being started, and I am sure that we will see even more startling growth in the next few decades. It is vital that we re-examine the way we train and release leaders so that these new churches have the best possible biblical foundation. This series is our contribution to equipping tomorrow's leaders with the eternal truths that they need.

Colin Dye

CONTENTS

Introduction   7

Part One   The Father's Priority   9

Part Two   Praise and Worship   21

Part Three   Worship in the Old Testament   33

Part Four   Worship in the Psalms   47

Part Five   Worship in the New Testament   59

Part Six   Service and Worship   73

Part Seven   Giving and Worship   83

Part Eight   Rejoicing and Worship   95

Part Nine   The Holy Spirit and Worship   107

Activities for individuals and small groups   123

INTRODUCTION

There is probably a greater diversity of public worship today than at any time in church history.

As recently as thirty years ago, most Anglican worship was based around the 1662 Prayer Book, most Roman Catholic worship was in Latin, and most Free Churches used the 'hymn-prayer sandwich'. Nearly all services were led by the recognised minister, the organist ruled supreme, and there was no leading role for women. Although there were different denominational hymn books, they contained very similar hymns – few churches sang any modern hymns or choruses.

In the last thirty years, however, there has been a revolution in worship. For example, services have become more informal; they are led by more people and many musical instruments; and they use modern liturgy and a mixture of contemporary and traditional songs.

Although these changes have reflected the increased informality in western society and the musical tastes of the post-Beatle generation, they have also been a response to the genuine work of the Holy Spirit through 'Charismatic Renewal'.

As a result of this, there has been a great deal of discussion (and disagreement) about the place of spiritual gifts, the role of women, the balance between prepared liturgy and spontaneity, the use of dance and drama, the position of the Lord's Supper, different forms of worship, acceptable styles of music, and so on.

Much less attention, however, has been paid to the biblical principles which undergird worship. By concentrating on form rather than substance, on modern details rather than scriptural principles, some congregations have put the proverbial cart before the biblical horse.

This, therefore, is a book for believers who are eager to study God's Word to learn about worship in spirit and truth; it is a book for Christians who want to go behind the debates about style and format to establish what the Bible means by worship and to discover God's eternal principles about the way he wants us to respond to his grace.

Please ensure that you read all the references – and tick the margin boxes as you go along to show that you have. Answer every question and think through each point as it is made. Before moving on to a new section, think carefully about the implications of what you have studied. Please allow God to speak to you as you study his Word.

At the end of the book, there is some activity material and questions. Please make sure that you study Parts 1–9 before beginning to work through the activities, as this will ensure that you have an overview of the biblical teaching about worship before you try to apply the details of any one aspect. These questions will help you to grasp and apply the scriptural material that you have studied.

You will also be able to use the activity pages when you teach the material to small groups. Please feel free to photocopy these pages and distribute them to any group you are leading. Although you should work through all the questions when you are studying on your own, please don't expect a small group to cover all the material.

By the time you finish this book, I pray you will have begun to appreciate that biblical worship is much, much more than what you do in church on a Sunday, and to grasp that God wants your *every* word and deed to be motivated by holy fear and adoring love.

Even more than this, I pray that you will have been inspired to make the worship of God your number one priority. Feed your mind with his truth, fire your imagination with his beauty, free yourself to his love, follow his perfect example, and firmly devote your will to his purposes – enjoy God, and worship him fully in spirit and truth.

Colin Dye

PART ONE

the father's priority

The title of this, the twelfth book in the *Sword of the Spirit* series, is drawn from a single verse of Scripture, from Jesus' words to the sinful woman whom he met by the well in Sychar.

John 4 describes Jesus' evangelistic encounter with this lady, and John 4:1–26 □ we see in *Reaching the Lost* how he made contact with her by placing himself in her debt, how he aroused her curiosity by hinting at something which was more satisfying than her present experience, and how he challenged the issue which was at the heart of her life.

It seems that Jesus' challenge was too close for comfort, for – in verse 20 – the woman raised a religious 'red herring'. The Jews and the Samaritans had different ideas about religion, especially about the right place to worship, and she used the issue as a diversionary tactic.

Even so, Jesus did not ignore her question, and – in verses 21–24 – he dealt with her query in words which clarify for all time the Father's priority of worship.

Jesus' words to this promiscuous pagan reveal God's eternal heart to all sinful people. He declared that the Father is seeking true worshippers, that the Father is seeking sinful men and women who will worship him in spirit and truth.

As with much that we consider in this series, worship is entirely the Father's initiative. It is his will and his purpose; it is he who is actively seeking worshippers for himself, eagerly drawing believers together to worship him, firmly persuading us that this is his will for our lives.

This means that true worship is always a human response to a divine initiative and never merely a human action to attract divine attention. This is precisely what we see throughout this series in so many other areas of 'the Word and the Spirit'.

It is God who walks in the garden of Eden seeking the sinful Adam and Eve and offers them blood-stained clothes of grace. It is God who speaks to Noah, covenants with him, keeps his family safe in a time of judgement, and inspires him to worship. It is God who calls Abram and draws him to Canaan. It is God who leads Israel from Egypt, across the Red Sea, through the desert and into the Promised Land.

John 12:32 ☐

And, supremely, it is God who, in Christ on the cross, draws all people to himself – we see this in John 12:32.

The ancient covenant promise, 'You will be my people and I will be your God' runs like a thread from Genesis to Revelation, as the Bible repeatedly underlines the Father's efforts to initiate, restore and maintain fellowship with his children.

Truly God is like the father in Jesus' parable of the prodigal son who, when he sees his son afar off, rushes to meet him and welcome him home with shouts of joy and extravagant celebrations.

Worship – in spirit

Worship 'in spirit' is always a stuttering prodigal response to a personal experience of the Father's gracious love, and it rises within people only when the Holy Spirit touches their human spirits.

On their own, careful rituals and set formulae cannot produce worship in spirit. For example, we can have great songs and gifted musicians, helpful techniques and culturally relevant styles, a well-prepared order of service and wise leaders, but we will not worship God in spirit until the Father draws us to himself and the Holy Spirit touches our human spirits.

Our singing, praying, praising, dancing, meditating, and so on, may lead to worship, but true worship will not occur until our spirits have been drawn by God to the Father and have been ignited by the work of the Spirit of truth.

This is not a book about modern forms of worship and contemporary techniques in leading worship; and it does not advocate a particular style of worship – for the New Testament never prescribes any techniques or asks for special forms. Instead, it is a book which looks at the Bible to find the way that the Father graciously draws people to himself, and to consider how he expects us to respond to his love.

Worship – in truth

In his struggle with the devil on a high mountain, recorded in Matthew 4:10, Jesus made it clear whom we should worship and whom we should serve. It is the one true God of the Bible, the God of Abraham and Isaac, the living God whom Jesus perfectly revealed.

Matthew 4:10 ☐

Exodus 20:3–5 shows that God's first two commandments to Israel demand exclusive worship. The first shows whom we must worship exclusively, and the second reveals how we should worship him exclusively. We must recognise, however, that there are two aspects to putting the true God before all other gods:

Exodus 20:3–5 ☐

- *we must not honour or adore anything more than the true God*

- *we must know the true God correctly if we are to honour and adore him above all else*

Just as we cannot worship God 'in spirit' if we have not been touched by the Spirit, so we cannot worship him 'in truth' if we do not know the truth about him. Worship 'in spirit' should be our eager response to what God has done in creation and salvation, and worship 'in truth' depends on us knowing the Father, the Son and the Spirit in the fullness of the biblical revelation.

True worship is not an aimless emotional activity, it is an action which is tightly focused on the one true God. If we are really to worship *him* in spirit and truth we must make every effort to know *him* better. This means that we must keep on studying his self-revelation to the people of Israel; that we must keep on meditating on all the divine attributes which he reveals in his written word; and that we must keep on gazing at his wonderful self-revelation in Jesus.

When we grasp the Father's great story of salvation, ponder on his unbreakable covenants, wonder at him being 'lifted up' for humanity, appreciate his infinite grace and mercy, and so on, we surely cannot help but start to worship him in spirit and truth.

Worship – with confession

Whenever we look closely at God and consider his purposes, we are bound to be drawn by him first to a place of confession. Like the prophet in Isaiah 6:5, we appreciate the truth of our own sinfulness only when we stare at God's absolute holiness, the truth of our fickleness only when we face his faithfulness, the truth of our guilt only when we gaze at his grace, and so on.

Isaiah 6:5 ☐

Of course, we worship God not only because of who he is, but also because of what he has done and is doing. The God of the Bible is the God who intervenes in history and breaks into human lives. He is the living God who speaks and saves, who heals and delivers, who judges, conquers and forgives.

He is the God who acts as well as the God who is, and his intrinsic goodness, faithfulness, justice, love, wisdom, patience and mercy are etched in mighty works throughout the whole Bible – and in our lives. Whenever we consider the mighty deeds of God (the mercies which are mentioned in Romans 12:1) we should be drawn to worship him in spirit and truth.

Romans 12:1 ☐

Worship – our first priority

In Mark 12:28–34, Jesus crystallises all God's commandments into two, and explains that loving the Lord, the only God, with every part of our being is the most important divine commandment. If God is to be 'the Lord' of our lives, worship must be our number one priority.

Mark 12:28–34 ☐

Jesus then shows that God's second requirement for our lives is serving others with the passion that we have for ourselves. This establishes two vital principles:

- *worshipping God and serving others are closely linked in God's purposes*

- *worshipping God comes first; serving others comes second*

According to Jesus, worship is God's chief purpose for humanity: he has created us to worship and enjoy him, and he has redeemed us to worship and enjoy him. Service flows from worship, and is based in worship, but it is not a substitute for worship. We must take care that our godly activities do not become the enemy of our godly adoration.

The Old Testament priests and levites were set apart to serve God, and their ministry to him took precedence over all their other work. Ezekiel's eschatological vision of the 'new temple' shows that the same principle will still apply at the end of time: Ezekiel 44:15 prophesies that the priests will still be called essentially to approach God and to minister personally to him.

Ezekiel 44:15 ☐

This means we must make sure that we are not so busy serving others, and responding to their genuine needs, that we neglect to minister personally to God in praise and worship.

Worship – with sincerity

True worship can come only from a sincere heart. Passages like Psalm 24:4; 50:8–23; 51:16–19; Proverbs 15:8; 21:27; Isaiah 1:11–20; 29:13; 58:1–14; 66:1–4; Jeremiah 6:20; 7:21–28; Hosea 8:11–13; Amos 5:21–24; Micah 6:6–8 and Matthew 15:7–8 make it plain that God hates any hint of religious pretence.

Psalm 24:4 ☐
50:8–23 ☐
51:16–19 ☐

Proverbs 15:8 ☐
21:27 ☐

Isaiah 1:11–20 ☐
29:13 ☐
58:1–14 ☐
66:1–4 ☐

Instead, God is looking for practical actions in his worshippers, not for symbolic gestures, for inner purity, and not for outer ritual. Through the Psalms, God calls his people to approach him with clean hands, a pure heart, a broken and contrite spirit. Hebrews 10:19–22 underlines that this is possible only through the blood of Jesus – and we study this in *Salvation by Grace*.

Jeremiah 6:20 ☐
7:21–28 ☐

Hosea 8:11–13 ☐

Amos 5:21–24 ☐

Micah 6:6–8 ☐

Matthew 15:7–8 ☐

We focus on Philippians 3:3 in Part Nine, but we should recognise here that our confidence in offering worship which is true, pleasing and acceptable must come from our dependence on the Spirit and not from any confidence in ourselves.

Hebrews
10:19–22 ☐

Philippians 3:3 ☐

Worship – with expectation

As true worship is always a human response to God's gracious initiative, we can move towards worship with the expectation that we will experience the reality of God when we worship in spirit and truth.

We will see in Parts Three and Five how God's people – in both the Old and the New Testament – knew that they would meet with God when they came together in worship. They expected that they would feel his loving touch, and hear his holy words, because they were coming to worship *in response to his call*.

Every time Moses went into the tabernacle, he knew that he had been summoned to meet the all-powerful, all-knowing, miracle-working God, and that the presence of God would be so great it would make his face glow with reflected divine glory.

Later, whenever the high priests entered the holy of holies on the God-appointed Day of Atonement, they stepped behind the curtain with a genuine sense of holy fear – because they knew that they were entering into the localised presence of the most Holy God.

It was the same in the early church. The first believers were filled with holy expectation when they met to worship God because they knew that some of them had dropped dead in his presence, that others had risen from the dead through his presence, and that at least two of their buildings had literally shaken with his presence.

When the first believers gathered together to worship, they knew that the temple curtain had been torn in two at Christ's death, and that – like Moses and the high priests – they would be entering the holiest place. They knew that they were being drawn into the terrible-yet-gracious presence of God, and so were sure that something extraordinary was bound to happen again!

Worship – our relationship

As we will see in Part Eight, by calling us to worship him God is calling us to enjoy him, to rejoice in his presence, to join with the Father, the Son and the Spirit in their eternal enjoyment of each other.

This means that the goal of our worship is always the presence of the triune God, that our call to worship is always a call to a deeper relationship with God, and that worship is the right expression of our redeemed relationship with God.

In the Old Testament, as we will see in Part Three, true worship takes place in the secret place of the tabernacle and temple, in the holy of holies behind the veil – in the tangible, localised presence of

God on earth. We will see in Part Five that the New Testament applies these pictures of worship to stress that believers are – both individually and corporately – tabernacles and temples of the Spirit which are set apart for worship.

The Father desires our communion and seeks our worship – this is why he has made and redeemed us. This 'relational worship' is fundamental to the whole concept of being 'God's children': it recognises who he is and what he has made us, and is an essential part of our relationship with him. As we recognise who God is in the fullness of his nature, and give him the worship due to his name, so we grow in our relationship with God.

But we do not worship God with a selfish purpose in mind; rather, we worship God to bless him. He loves and desires our fellowship – this is why he has made and redeemed us – and he deeply enjoys our intimate company and conversation.

It is God's main desire for us to enjoy each other in the secret place, to enter fully into each other's presence, to develop an enduring face-to-face relationship, to worship him in spirit and truth.

THE LEADER OF WORSHIP

As genuine worship is essentially a human response to a divine initiative, it should be clear that worship in spirit and truth must always be led and directed by God himself.

When Moses pleaded with Pharaoh to allow the Israelites to spend a few days in the wilderness worshipping God, he had to explain to the Egyptian ruler that they would not know what form of worship they would offer God until they reached the designated place of worship.

Exodus 10:24–26 establishes the important biblical principle that, if God's people really want to please the living God in worship, they must allow him personally to direct their worship.

Exodus 10:24–26 □

This means that true Christian worship has only one real leader – God, in Christ, through the Spirit. All human 'leaders' of worship are merely 'under-leaders' who are called to pass on God's personal direction for worship and not their own ideas and tastes.

When God draws his people to worship him, he himself is present among them as they worship him. He is not a passive inspector who assesses their worship to check that it meets his requirements; instead, by the Spirit, he is an active participant in the worship. He speaks by his Spirit into the hearts of worshipping men and women and makes his holy presence known. He teaches, guides, rebukes and comforts them whenever they respond to his call to worship him in spirit and truth.

In worship, we do not only read about God theoretically in the Scriptures, we know him experientially as he reveals himself in our spirits in a great host of ways. We will see in Part Three how, in Old Testament times, God revealed his glory at the hour of worship. And we see in *Glory in the Church* how God still wants to reveal his glory to the world through the church – we consider this fully in Parts Six, Seven and Eight.

This means that we do not only celebrate Jesus as our Saviour and Redeemer when we worship, we also experience him as our Prophet, Priest and King. By the Spirit, Jesus comes among us in our worship to teach us about righteousness, to feed and sanctify us with his word of life, and to give us his power to do what is right.

We see throughout this *Sword of the Spirit* series that God always acts self-consistently, that he is *always* true to *every* aspect of his nature. This means that when he comes among us in worship he is present in the fullness of every aspect of his character.

As a result, we should expect to experience God's love *and* his grace, his truth *and* his mercy, his comfort *and* his power, his liberty *and* his self-discipline, his healing *and* his humility, and so on, whenever we respond to his call to worship.

Because God himself is with us when we worship, he is with us in all his power, all his love, all his grace, all his truth. And because God is leading and directing us when we worship, we should surely expect that every aspect of his nature will be revealed through the worship.

This suggests that miracles of grace and power should be the rule, not the exception, when we worship in spirit and truth, that healings of the body and the mind should be a normal occurrence, and that gifts of grace and divine humility should be almost commonplace.

God decides

The biblical principle that 'God's people must allow God to direct their worship if they are to please him with their worship' means that he alone decides which men and women, and what natural and spiritual gifts, are to be used in worship.

In public church worship, people preach, prophesy, sing, pray, give, arrange flowers, read the Scriptures, play an instrument, polish pews, collect hymn-books, greet visitors, and so on, only as they are personally called and directed by the real leader of the worship. This ensures that there is no room for self-promotion through worship, and no place for establishing a human reputation. Only the holy God is glorified in worship which is offered in spirit and truth.

Every aspect of public church worship is meant to demonstrate that God is the only initiator and ultimate leader of the worship:

- *every spiritual gift should reveal that Christ is in complete control; that he gives what he chooses, when he chooses, how he chooses, through whom he chooses*

- *every spoken word should breathe God's life into the worship, and build the worshippers, because the speaker has been inspired to speak only by the life-giving Spirit*

- *every discreet act of service should ignite the worship with God's love and humility, because the servant has been moved to act only by God's self-effacing Spirit*

- *every mighty miracle should thrill and awe the worshippers because it points only to God's compassion and mercy, and not to a human technique or self-seeking messenger*

OUR RESPONSE

As we will see in Part Three, God's people in the Old Testament came before God in worship not only to praise and adore him but also to be cleansed and transformed by him. They knew that they could not stand in the holy presence of Almighty God and remain the same. In fact, we can almost say that we cannot have worshipped in spirit and truth if we have not been changed through the worship.

Just as true worship begins in holy expectancy, so it ends in holy obedience. Worship is not a means of escape from the rigours of the world; rather, it is a confrontation with God's call to serve him in the world. Like the prophet in Isaiah 6:8, it is when we worship God, and have been cleansed and transformed by him, that we most recognise our need to respond to God's call to serve him with gospel obedience.

Isaiah 6:8 ☐

As we have seen, our worship of God may have to come first, but it must also always lead to our service of others. On top of this, authentic worship also draws us into the spiritual dimension and exposes us to the realities of the invisible world. It is as we worship in spirit and truth that we are impelled to share with Christ in the application of his victory against demonic powers at every level of life.

This suggests that there is a always a natural spiritual progression at work in true worship. For example:

- *God calls us, by the Spirit, to worship him*

- *we respond to God's summons*

- *we come face-to-face with God in the worship*

- *we follow his leading and direction as to how we worship*

- *we are changed by his presence during the worship*

- *we receive his orders for service, and his equipping to serve, while we worship*

- *we go from worship to love God, to serve others, and to apply Christ's victory*

Focusing on God

It should be clear that, if worship is our response to God's call, we must 'hear' his call to be able to respond. We consider this throughout *Listening to God*, and study how God communicates with his people and how we can learn to recognise his way of 'speaking' to us today.

Once we are have 'heard' or 'sensed' God's call to worship, we need to turn all our attention on him. This involves stilling all our humanly-initiated activities and concentrating hard on him.

Many believers confine this 'human stilling' and God focusing to the few minutes before a public worship service; but this 'stilling and focusing' should always be part of the fabric of the lives of every believer. As we see in *Listening to God*, we are called to develop a continuous, listening life-style so that all our words and deeds have their source in God.

If we carry out the ordinary business of our lives in our own strength and wisdom, we will tend to do the same when we gather together to worship. But if we are always thoroughly alert to God's prompting – at home and at work, while travelling and resting, with our family and friends, and so on – we will be bound to have the same divine sensitivity when we come together with other believers to worship.

Praising God

We will see in Parts Two to Five that God has always drawn his people into worship by encouraging them to praise both him and his mighty works.

The book of Psalms, for example, repeatedly urges God's Old Testament people to praise the Lord, and Hebrews 13:15 and 1 Peter 2:5–9 instruct God's new covenant people to offer him the sacrifice of praise and to declare his wonderful deeds – we focus on this in Part Eight.

Hebrews 13:15 ☐

1 Peter 2:5–9 ☐

Praise is important not only because it proclaims God's greatness, but also because it involves our emotions and feelings. True worship always involves the whole human personality; it includes our mind, our emotions, our body and our will; it embraces our words, our attitudes, our life-style – everything that we are and have.

God calls us with his whole being, with every aspect of his divine nature; he calls us, therefore, to respond to him with our whole beings, with every aspect of our redeemed nature. We are to present our whole human personality to God and offer him everything on the altar of worship. Nothing less is true worship, and nothing less is God's plan.

For his sake and for our sake, he summons us to worship him in spirit and truth.

PART TWO

praise and worship

Some believers use the word 'worship' without understanding what it really means. They usually think about it in terms of their own congregation's public worship rather than its biblical meaning. They assume that worship means what they do during a Sunday service, and that whatever they do in a Sunday service must be worship.

This results in one group of believers associating worship with, for example, free spontaneity and loud noise, while another group associates it with set liturgy and quiet reverence. If, however, we are to understand God's biblical call to worship him in spirit and truth, we must move beyond the modern arguments about different forms of worship and examine what the Scriptures mean by worshipping God.

The Bible uses a large number of Hebrew and Greek words to define and describe 'worship', but the essential context in both the Old and the New Testaments is always 'active service'.

The Hebrew word *abodah* and the Greek word *latreia* are the commonest scriptural words for 'worship', and they both originally signify the work of slaves or servants.

SERVICE

Most people today believe that 'worship' means one thing and that 'service' means something quite different (even though they commonly speak about 'worship services'). They assume that 'worship' means spiritual activities like singing and praying, and that 'service' means practical actions like sweeping floors, arranging chairs, and so on.

The Bible, however, makes no such distinction. As far as the Scriptures are concerned, our worship of God is our service of God; the way that we serve him is the way that we worship him.

Abodah

The Hebrew noun *abodah* is translated in some English versions of the Bible as 'work', in others as 'worship', and in most as 'service'. It is the same with the verb *abad*, which is rendered as either 'to work', 'to worship' or 'to serve'.

Genesis 14:4; 15:13–14; 25:23; 29:15–30 and Exodus 1:14 show that the *abodah* word-group originally referred to the practical work of slaves or hired servants.

Whenever the Scriptures use *abad* or *abodah* with a human object, it always refers to either a servile attitude or a serving action: we see this, for example, in Exodus 21:2; Jeremiah 40:9 and Ezekiel 48:18–19.

The Old Testament, however, almost always uses *abad* and *abodah* to describe the way that God's people rightly serve the true God or wrongly serve false gods.

It is important that our understanding of 'worship in spirit and truth' is based on the recognition that biblical worship embraces both *practical actions* and *spiritual activities*. The Old Testament uses the *abodah* word-group, for example:

- *to call people to serve/worship God* – Exodus 3:12; 7:16; 8:1, 20; 9:1, 13; 23:25; Deuteronomy 10:12; 11:13; Joshua 24:14–16; Psalm 2:11; 100:2; Jeremiah 30:9; Zephaniah 3:9

- *to call people away from serving/worshipping false gods* – Deuteronomy 7:16; 28:14; Jeremiah 25:6; 35:15

Genesis 14:4 ☐
15:13–14 ☐
25:23 ☐
29:15–30 ☐

Exodus 1:14 ☐
21:2 ☐

Jeremiah 40:9 ☐

Ezekiel 48:18–19 ☐

Exodus 3:12 ☐
7:16 ☐
8:1, 20 ☐
9:1, 13 ☐
23:25 ☐

Deuteronomy
10:12 ☐
11:13 ☐

Joshua 24:14–16 ☐

Psalm 2:11 ☐
100:2 ☐

Jeremiah 30:9 ☐

Zephaniah 3:9 ☐

Deuteronomy
7:16 ☐
28:14 ☐

Jeremiah 25:6 ☐
35:15 ☐

- *to describe practical actions which contribute to the service/ worship of God* – Exodus 36:1–5; Numbers 3:7–8; 4:23–28, 47– 49; 7:6–9; 1 Chronicles 28:20–21; 2 Chronicles 24:12

- *to describe spiritual activities which contribute to the service/ worship of God* – Numbers 8:11, 19–26; 18:6–7; 1 Chronicles 23:24–32

- *to describe musical contributions to the service/worship of God* – 1 Chronicles 25:1–8

- *to describe specific spiritual ceremonies* – Exodus 12:25–26; 2 Chronicles 35:1–19

The wide meaning of the *abodah* word-group is particularly clear in 2 Chronicles 35. This chapter describes a Passover 'worship/service' which was held in Jerusalem by king Josiah.

- *verses 2–3* record how Josiah encouraged the priests in their duties of service and the levites in their service of God and his people

- *verses 4–14* describe the practical preparations for the service by both the levites and the lay people

- *verses 15–16* show that the singers and gatekeepers (the Old Testament equivalent of modern day stewards) were deemed to be as involved in the worship/service as the priests and levites

This suggests both that careful preparation for a God-directed worship service is as much worship/service to God as the worship service itself, and that the practical actions of the 'gatekeepers' and generous giving of the 'lay people' are as much an act of service/ worship as the musical contributions of the 'singers' and spiritual activities of the 'priests and levites'.

Latreia

Latreia, 'service', and *latreuo*, 'to serve', are the Greek equivalents of *abodah* and *abad*. Again, they originally signify the hired service of a slave or servant, but are mainly used in the New Testament to describe human service or worship of God.

This word group is used, for example, in Matthew 4:10; Luke 1:74; 2:37; 4:8; Acts 7:7; 24:14; 26:7; 27:23; Romans 1:9; 9:4; 12:1;

Exodus 36:1–5 ☐

Numbers 3:7–8 ☐
4:23–28 ☐
4:47–49 ☐
7:6–9 ☐

1 Chronicles
28:20–21 ☐

2 Chronicles
24:12 ☐

Numbers 8:11 ☐
8:19–26 ☐
18:6–7 ☐

1 Chronicles
23:24–32 ☐

Exodus 12:25–26 ☐

1 Chronicles
25:1–8 ☐

2 Chronicles
35:1–19 ☐

Matthew 4:10 ☐

Luke 1:74 ☐
2:37 ☐
4:8 ☐

Acts 7:7 ☐
24:14 ☐
26:7 ☐
27:23 ☐

Romans 1:9 ☐
9:4 ☐
12:1 ☐

Philippians 3:3 ☐

2 Timothy 1:3 ☐

Hebrews 8:5 ☐

9:1, 6, 14 ☐

10:2 ☐

12:28 ☐

Revelation 7:15 ☐

22:3 ☐

Romans 12:1 ☐

Philippians 3:3; 2 Timothy 1:3; Hebrews 8:5; 9:1, 6, 14; 10:2; 12:28; Revelation 7:15 and 22:3.

A careful reading of these passages shows the Scriptures use one-and-the-same word to describe spiritual 'worship' in the tabernacle, temple, heaven, and so on, and practical 'service' in everyday life.

The use of *latreia* in Romans 12:1 encapsulates both of these meanings: we are called to present our bodies as a living sacrifice to God in *everything* that we do: there is no distinction between so-called 'spiritual' and 'secular' activities – our work is our worship, and worship is our work.

BOWING DOWN

If the *abodah* and *latreia* word-groups emphasise the relationship between worship and service, the *shachah* and *proskuneo* word-groups stress that the essence of worship/service is bowing down before God.

The Hebrew word *shachah* and the Greek word *proskuneo* are normally translated as 'worship', and they both reveal that God's servants must have an attitude of bowing before him if they are to offer the worship/service that he expects and deserves.

Shachah literally means 'to bow self down', and *proskuneo* literally means 'to kiss towards'. Together they show that our worship/service should spring from reverential fear and adoring awe and wonder.

These words make it plain that God is not looking principally for the outward activities of praying, praising, singing, serving, and so on; rather, he is mainly seeking the inner attitudes of reverential fear and adoring love. Although we should try to ensure that our public worship is culturally relevant, discussions and disagreements about different forms of worship miss the point of God's call.

John 4:20–24 ☐

Jesus' conversation with the Samaritan woman, in John 4:1–24, shows that the outward aspects of worship are not its essence. *Proskuneo* is used seven times in John 4:20–24 to underline that God is more concerned with the correct inner attitude of 'kissing towards' him, than with issues of outward place and form.

Shachah

Shachah is often used literally in the Old Testament to show that God's people physically prostrated themselves when they came before him: they either bowed their heads, or knelt, or fell face-forward to the ground. We see this, for example, in Genesis 24:26–28; Exodus 4:31; 12:27; 34:8; 1 Chronicles 29:20; 2 Chronicles 20:18; 29:30; Nehemiah 8:6; Job 1:20 and Psalm 95:6.

More usually, however, *shachah* is used to show that God's people were called to have an inner attitude of reverent fear and adoring love when they came before God. We see this, for example, in Genesis 22:5; Exodus 24:1; Deuteronomy 26:10; 1 Samuel 1:28; 1 Chronicles 16:29; Nehemiah 9:3; Psalm 96:9 and 99:5.

Because *shachah* points essentially to the inner attitude of worship/ service, it is commonly used in the Old Testament in conjunction with another verb which describes the accompanying outward action of worship/service. For example,

- *bowing and worship* – Genesis 24:26, 48; Exodus 4:31

- *sacrifice and worship* – Exodus 32:8; 1 Samuel 1:3; 2 Kings 17:36

- *service and worship* – Deuteronomy 8:19

- *praise and worship* – 2 Chronicles 7:3; Psalm 66:4

- *confession and worship* – Nehemiah 9:3

- *eating and worship* – Psalm 22:29

The constant biblical link between *shachah* and, for example, praise, service and sacrifice, demonstrates the importance of the motivating attitude. Praise which does not flow from reverence and love does not impress God. Service which is not motivated by awe and wonder does not please God. Sacrifice which does not stem from fear and devotion is not acceptable to God – and so on.

Proskuneo

It is much the same with *proskuneo*, 'to kiss towards', in the New Testament. Sometimes this word is used literally to describe a physical action which signifies reverent fear and adoring love; for example,

Genesis 24:26–28
Exodus 4:31
12:27
34:8
1 Chronicles 29:20
2 Chronicles 20:18
29:30
Nehemiah 8:6
Job 1:20
Psalm 95:6
Genesis 22:5
Exodus 24:1
Deuteronomy 26:10
1 Samuel 1:28
1 Chronicles 16:29
Nehemiah 9:3
Psalm 96:9
99:5
Genesis 24:26
24:48
Exodus 4:31
32:8
1 Samuel 1:3
2 Kings 17:36
Deuteronomy 8:19
2 Chronicles 7:3
Psalm 66:4
Nehemiah 9:3
Psalm 22:29

Matthew 2:11 ☐
       4:9 ☐
      28:9 ☐

Mark 15:19 ☐

Acts 10:25 ☐

1 Corinthians
      14:25 ☐

Revelation 7:11 ☐
       11:16 ☐
     19:4, 10 ☐
        22:8 ☐

Matthew 8:2 ☐
      9:18 ☐
     14:33 ☐
     15:25 ☐
     18:26 ☐

Mark 5:6 ☐

John 4:23–24 ☐
       9:38 ☐

Acts 24:11 ☐

Revelation 4:10 ☐

Matthew 15:9 ☐

Mark 7:7 ☐

Acts 16:14 ☐
      18:7, 13 ☐
       19:27 ☐

Romans 1:25 ☐

Acts 17:23 ☐

Matthew 2:11; 4:9; 28:9; Mark 15:19; Acts 10:25; 1 Corinthians 14:25; Revelation 7:11; 11:16; 19:4, 10 and 22:8.

Usually, however, *proskuneo* is used to describe the inner heart attitude of reverence and adoration. We see this, for example, in Matthew 8:2; 9:18; 14:33; 15:25; 18:26; Mark 5:6; John 4:23–24; 9:38; Acts 24:11 and Revelation 4:10.

Other words

Three other Greek words are translated as 'to worship' in most English versions of the New Testament:

- *sebomai* means 'to revere', and is used in Matthew 15:9; Mark 7:7; Acts 16:14; 18:7, 13 and 19:27

- *sebazomai* means 'to venerate', and is used in Romans 1:25

- *eusebeo* means 'to be reverential', and is used in Acts 17:23

As with *proskuneo*, these three words stress an inner feeling of awe or devotion rather than an outer action.

We have seen that the Bible often uses the word 'worship', but it never defines 'worship'; however, the different Hebrew and Greek words for worship suggest that it is a serving action which stems from an attitude of reverent fear and loving adoration.

We can say, therefore, that worship is a direct acknowledgement to God of his nature, attributes, ways and claims which is both felt internally and is also expressed in spiritual and practical actions.

PRAISE

The Bible not only uses several Greek and Hebrew words to paint a composite picture of scriptural worship, it also uses many different words for praise to present another multi-faceted activity.

Just as we need to broaden our modern understanding of worship to include practical service and inner attitudes, so we need to recognise that praise is more than singing loud songs about God.

In the Old Testament, 'praise' usually means an act of homage or worship which is offered to God by his creatures – generally, but not always, by men and women. The different Hebrew words which are translated as 'praise' all refer to particular types of worship, and our understanding of praise must embrace them all.

Halal

Halal is the commonest Hebrew verb to be translated as 'to praise', and basically means 'to shout for joy'. It seems that *halal* was originally used to refer to the wail of grief at the death of a sacrifice, but that it then became the word used to describe the shout of joy at God's acceptance of the sacrifice.

The essence of *halal* is making a loud noise, and it is used in the Old Testament to describe praise about-or-to:

- *a man or woman* – Genesis 12:15; Proverbs 27:2; 28:4; 31:28–31; 2 Samuel 14:25

- *false gods* – Judges 16:24

- *God* – 1 Chronicles 16:36; 2 Chronicles 5:13; 20:19–21; 30:21; Ezra 3:10–11; Nehemiah 5:13; Psalm 22:23; 35:18; 63:5; 69:30–34; 119:164; 148:1; 150:1–6; Isaiah 62:9; Jeremiah 20:13

- *the name of God* – Psalm 69:30; 74:21; 145:2; 148:5; Joel 2:26

- *the word of God* – Psalm 56:4, 10

As we will see in Part Three, praise and worship in Old Testament times was usually a corporate activity, and the biblical emphasis on congregational *halal* is plain in passages like Judges 16:24; 1 Chronicles 16:36; 23:5; 2 Chronicles 23:12; 30:21; Ezra 3:11; Nehemiah 5:13; Psalm 22:22; 35:18; 102:18; 107:32; 109:30 and 117:1.

Today, we often associate praise with thanksgiving. Interestingly, of all the different Hebrew words for praise, only *halal* is linked to thanksgiving. It seems that when the people wanted to thank God in praise, they thanked him with great shouts of joy. We see this, for example, in 1 Chronicles 16:4; 23:30; 25:3; 29:13 and Nehemiah 12:24.

The expression *Hallelujah*, 'Praise the Lord', is used in Psalm 104:35 and 135:3, at the beginnings of Psalms 106; 111; 112; 113; 135; 146–149, and at the ends of Psalms 104–106; 113; 115–117; 135; 146–150.

Genesis 12:15
Proverbs 27:2
28:4
31:28–31
2 Samuel 14:25
Judges 16:24
1 Chronicles
16:36
2 Chronicles 5:13
20:19–21
30:21
Ezra 3:10–11
Nehemiah 5:13
Psalm 22:23
35:18
63:5
69:30–34
119:164
148:1
150:1–6
Isaiah 62:9
Jeremiah 20:13
Psalm 69:30
74:21
145:2
148:5
Joel 2:26
Psalm 56:4, 10
Judges 16:24
1 Chronicles 23:5
2 Chronicles
23:12
30:21
Psalm 22:22
35:18
102:18
107:32
109:30
117:1
1 Chronicles 16:4
23:30
25:3
29:13
Nehemiah 12:24
Psalm 104:35
135:3

Lamentations
    3:53 ☐

1 Kings 8:33–35 ☐

2 Chronicles
    6:24–26 ☐

Job 40:14 ☐

Psalm 32:5 ☐

2 Samuel 22:50 ☐

1 Chronicles
    16:4–8 ☐

Psalm 18:49 ☐
    30:12 ☐
    136:1–20 ☐

1 Chronicles
    29:13 ☐

2 Chronicles 31:2 ☐

Ezra 3:11 ☐

Nehemiah 12:24 ☐

Genesis 29:35 ☐

2 Chronicles 7:3 ☐

Psalm 9:1 ☐
    42:5 ☐
    44:8 ☐
    54:6 ☐
    57:9 ☐
    86:12 ☐
    108:3 ☐
    118:28 ☐
    138:1–2 ☐

Isaiah 12:1–4 ☐
    25:1 ☐
    38:19 ☐

Jeremiah 33:11 ☐

Yadah

The Hebrew verb *yadah* is usually translated as to praise, but its literal meaning is 'to throw' – as in Lamentations 3:53.

This may seem puzzling, but – in many parts of the world – people still praise others by throwing things at them: for example, Americans praise their returning heroes by showering them with 'ticker-tape', and Europeans praise newly-married couples by throwing confetti, flower petals and rice over them.

Yadah is used in two complementary ways to suggest that:

- *gestures of either the body or the spirit accompany the praise offered by God's people*
- *praise is essentially confessional or declaratory*

Some versions of the Bible translate *yadah* as 'confess' (in, for example, 1 Kings 8:33–35; 2 Chronicles 6:24–26; Job 40:14 and Psalm 32:5) and as 'give thanks' (in, for example, 2 Samuel 22:50; 1 Chronicles 16:4–8; Psalm 18:49; 30:12; 136:1–20). It is, however, exactly the same word that they translate elsewhere as 'praise'.

In several places, *yadah* is used in a sequence with *halal* – as in 1 Chronicles 29:13; 2 Chronicles 31:2; Ezra 3:11 and Nehemiah 12:24. In such passages, translators usually render *halal* as praise and *yadah* as give thanks to stress the distinction between the two words. These passages, however, show that God expects our praise to include both *halal* noise and *yadah* gestures of the body or spirit.

Every use of *yadah* implies both a gesture and a declaration, and we need to ensure that our understanding of praise includes gestures, and to recognise that our praising words can be in the form of a thanksgiving, or a confession, or a public declaration: it is all praise.

Yadah is used in the general sense of praise in, for example, Genesis 29:35; 2 Chronicles 7:3; Psalm 9:1; 42:5; 44:8; 54:6; 57:9; 86:12; 108:3; 118:28; 138:1–2; Isaiah 12:1–4; 25:1; 38:19 and Jeremiah 33:11.

Zamar

This verb comes from the 'hum' of a stringed instrument, and is used in the Old Testament when praise is associated with singing or the playing of a musical instrument.

The noun *mizmor* is derived from *zamar*; and is the word for 'psalm'. It is used in the title of 57 Psalms to introduce 'a song which is sung to a musical accompaniment'.

Zamar is usually translated as 'to sing praise', and is used in, for example, Judges 5:3; 2 Samuel 22:50; Psalm 7:17; 9:11; 47:6; 61:8; 98:4; 108:1; 144:9; 147:7; 149:3 and Isaiah 12:5.

Shabach

This verb comes from a root which means 'to stroke, still or smooth', and is used in Psalms 8:2; 65:7; 89:9 and Proverbs 29:11 to describe the 'stilling' or 'calming' of anger, the sea and enemies. Elsewhere, *shabach* refers to 'soothing God with praises': it is used, for example, in Psalm 63:4; 117:1; 145:4; 147:12; Daniel 2:23; 4:34–37; 5:4, 23.

Shabach is usually translated as 'to praise', but some versions render it as 'bless', or 'laud', or 'glorify', or 'honour' – especially when it is used in a sequence with *halal*. This suggests that our praise should include times of *shabach* gentleness as well as outbursts of *halal* noise.

Todah

This noun is usually translated as 'thanksgiving', but is sometimes rendered as 'praise' – as, for example, in Psalms 42:4; 50:23 and 56:12.

While there is a great deal of overlap between worship, praise and thanksgiving, they can be distinguished in two ways.

- *Worship is the appreciation of God's being; praise is the appreciation of his nature; and thanksgiving is the appreciation of his activity.*

- *Worship is an all-embracing expression for every word, deed and attitude which flows from the acknowledgement of the supreme worth of God; praise refers essentially to a verbal declaration of appreciation about God; and thanksgiving refers to either a verbal declaration or a generous action which expresses gratitude for what God has done.*

This overlap is the main reason why words like *yadah* and *todah* are sometimes translated as praise and other times as thanksgiving. There is a distinction, but it is rarely significant.

Judges 5:3 ☐

2 Samuel 22:50 ☐

Psalm 7:17 ☐
9:11 ☐
47:6 ☐
61:8 ☐
98:4 ☐
108:1 ☐
144:9 ☐
147:7 ☐
149:3 ☐

Isaiah 12:5 ☐

Psalms 8:2 ☐
65:7 ☐
89:9 ☐

Proverbs 29:11 ☐

Psalm 63:4 ☐
117:1 ☐
145:4 ☐
147:12 ☐

Daniel 2:23 ☐
4:34–37 ☐
5:4 ☐
5:23 ☐

Psalm 42:4 ☐
50:23 ☐
56:12 ☐

Luke 2:13 ☐
2:20 ☐
19:37 ☐
24:53 ☐
Acts 2:47 ☐
3:8–9 ☐
Romans 15:11 ☐
Revelation 19:5 ☐
1 Corinthians
11:2 ☐
11:17–22 ☐
2 Corinthians
8:18 ☐
Ephesians
1:12–14 ☐
Philippians 1:11 ☐
4:8 ☐
1 Peter 1:7 ☐
2:14 ☐
Matthew 26:30 ☐
Mark 14:26 ☐
Acts 16:25 ☐
Hebrews 2:12 ☐
James 5:13 ☐
Matthew 11:25 ☐
Luke 10:21 ☐
Romans 14:11 ☐
15:9 ☐
Philippians 2:11 ☐
Revelation 3:5 ☐
Matthew 26:27 ☐
Mark 8:6 ☐
Luke 17:16 ☐
John 11:41 ☐
Acts 28:15 ☐
Romans 1:8 ☐
1 Corinthians
14:18 ☐
Ephesians 5:20 ☐
Colossians 1:3 ☐
2 Thessalonians
2:13 ☐
Revelation 11:17 ☐

New Testament words

Many different Greek words are translated in most English versions of the New Testament as 'to praise'. They each have slightly different meanings, and we need to have an understanding and practice of praise which embraces them all.

- *aineo*: this originally meant 'to narrate a story', but it is used in the New Testament to describe spoken praise to God – for example, Luke 2:13, 20; 19:37; 24:53; Acts 2:47; 3:8–9; Romans 15:11; Revelation 19:5

- *epaineo*: this means 'to commend' and refers to an enthusiastic spoken commendation – for example, 1 Corinthians 11:2, 17, 22; 2 Corinthians 8:18; Ephesians 1:12–14; Philippians 1:11; 4:8; 1 Peter 1:7; 2:14

- *humneo*: this Greek verb is the source of 'hymn' and means 'to sing praise' – it is used, for example, in Matthew 26:30; Mark 14:26; Acts 16:25 and Hebrews 2:12

- *psallo*: this means 'to twang a stringed instrument', and refers to making praise with a musical instrument – as in James 5:13

- *exomologeo*: this means 'to confess' and points to an open acknowledgement, celebration or declaration; some versions translate this as 'give thanks' but 'praise' is more accurate – it is used in Matthew 11:25; Luke 10:21; Romans 14:11; 15:9; Philippians 2:11 and Revelation 3:5

- *eucharisteo*: although this word literally means 'to give thanks', and is usually translated into English as such, it is actually the most common New Testament word for praise and is used in much the same way as *yadah*.

Eucharisteo describes the God-ward expression of joy and is one aspect of the fruit of the Spirit. It is used, for example, in Matthew 26:27; Mark 8:6; Luke 17:16; John 11:41; Acts 28:15; Romans 1:8; 1 Corinthians 14:18; Ephesians 5:20; Colossians 1:3; 2 Thessalonians 2:13; Revelation 11:17.

Many traditions of the church describe the Lord's Supper as the Eucharist because they consider the meal to be essentially an act of thanksgiving for Christ's death.

BIBLICAL PRAISE

The whole of the Bible is punctuated by outbursts of praise which seem to rise spontaneously from the basic mood of joy which characterises the life of God's people throughout the Scriptures.

The Bible makes it clear that God delights in his creation, and that all creation should express its joy in praise. We see this, for example, in Genesis 1; Psalm 90:14–16; 104:31; Proverbs 8:30–31; Job 38:4–7; Revelation 4:6–11.

Praise is one of the key distinguishing marks of God's people, and non-believers evidence their lack of faith by their refusal to praise. We see this in Romans 1:21; 1 Peter 2:9; Ephesians 1:3–14; Philippians 1:11 and Revelation 16:9.

The Bible shows that the coming of God's kingdom is marked by the restoration of deep joy and genuine praise to God's people, and to the whole creation – Isaiah 9:2; Psalm 96:11–13; Luke 2:13–14 and Revelation 5:9–14.

We will see in Part Three that the praise and worship in the tabernacle and temple was a foretaste of kingdom praise, and that it arose from the people's joy at being in the redeeming presence of God – we see this, for example, in Deuteronomy 27:7; Numbers 10:10 and Leviticus 23:40.

Job 1:21, however, shows that biblical praise does not only express a mood of joy, for the people were often commanded to rejoice before *Yahweh* whatever their feelings and circumstances – as in Deuteronomy 12:7; 16:11–12.

Careful arrangements were made for the temple praise, so it was not always spontaneous. Exodus 15:20; 2 Samuel 6:14; Psalm 42:4; 149:3 and 150 show that this involved psalms, shouts, processions, antiphonal singing, dancing and musical instruments.

We will see in Part Five that the first Christian believers continued to express their joy by joining in the temple worship – as in Luke 24:53 and Acts 3:1. Mark 2:22 suggests, however, that the experience of new life in Christ would need to express itself in new forms of praise.

Men and women who experienced the power of Jesus usually broke into spontaneous praise – we see this, for example, in Luke 18:43 and

---

Genesis 1 ☐

Psalm 90:14–16 ☐
104:31 ☐

Proverbs 8:30–31 ☐

Job 38:4–7 ☐

Revelation 4:6–11 ☐

Romans 1:21 ☐

1 Peter 2:9 ☐

Ephesians 1:3–14 ☐

Philippians 1:11 ☐

Revelation 16:9 ☐

Isaiah 9:2 ☐

Psalm 96:11–13 ☐

Luke 2:13–14 ☐

Revelation 5:9–14 ☐

Deuteronomy 27:7 ☐

Numbers 10:10 ☐

Leviticus 23:40 ☐

Job 1:21 ☐

Deuteronomy 12:7 ☐
16:11–12 ☐

Exodus 15:20 ☐

2 Samuel 6:14 ☐

Psalm 42:4 ☐
149:3 ☐
150 ☐

Luke 24:53 ☐

Acts 3:1 ☐

Mark 2:22 ☐

Luke 18:43 ☐

Mark 2:12 ☐

Acts 2:46 ☐
    3:8 ☐
    11:18 ☐
    16:25 ☐

Ephesians 1:1–14 ☐

Colossians 3:16 ☐

Matthew 26:30 ☐

1 Corinthians
    14:26 ☐

Colossians 3:16 ☐

Revelation 5:8–14 ☐

Luke 1:46–55 ☐
    1:68–79 ☐
    2:29–32 ☐

Hebrews 13:15 ☐

Leviticus 7:11–21 ☐

Deuteronomy
    26:1–11 ☐

Mark 2:12. And the New Testament records several outbursts of praise when people began to grasp or experience the power of God – for example, Acts 2:46; 3:8; 11:18; 16:25 and Ephesians 1:1–14.

Colossians 3:16 and Matthew 26:30 report that the first believers used the Old Testament Psalms in their praise and worship, and we consider these in Part Four. 1 Corinthians 14:26; Colossians 3:16 and Revelation 5:8–14 show that the early church also used new hymns in their praises; and Luke 1:46–55, 68–79; 2:29–32 and Acts 2:4–11 describes several new forms of prophetic praise.

The sacrifice of praise

Hebrews 13:15 mentions a 'sacrifice of praise'. This looks back to Leviticus 7:11–21, which established the place of thanksgiving in the Old Testament ritual sacrifices, and to Deuteronomy 26:1–11, which shows that gratitude is meant to be the fundamental motive behind the bringing of gifts to the altar.

In this chapter, we have examined the different scriptural words for praise and worship, and have begun to appreciate the breadth and depth of meaning in biblical praise and worship. We must keep this broad understanding in mind as we move on to consider worship/service throughout the Old and New Testaments, and to apply this to our lives today.

PART THREE

worship in the old testament

In the Old Testament, worship is the response of God's people to God's revelation of his nature; and the full nature of God – his holiness – determines the character of his people's response. For example:

- *because God is almighty and perfect, worship must respect his holiness*

- *because God is righteous and good, worship must face up to the problem of human sin*

- *because God is gracious and loving, the repentant worshipper can look for God's forgiveness and the promise of new life*

The precise way in which these ideas relate to each other varies from one occasion of worship to another, but all Old Testament worship begins with the recognition that *Yahweh* is who he is, and that his people are what they are – that he is holy and that they are not.

The different places, types and aspects of Old Testament worship all celebrate the many gracious ways in which God's sinful people can be made fit to encounter his holy presence and to experience his holy self.

PLACES OF WORSHIP

As we see in *Glory in the Church*, modern Christian places of worship are simply buildings where people can meet together. Their size, shape and location are determined more by social convenience than by spiritual considerations. Christians can worship anywhere, and many groups meet for worship in schools, public halls, and even the open air.

It was different in the Old Testament. Worship was offered only at a specific place where God had previously revealed himself in some tangible way. The people assumed that God's holiness could safely interact with the sinful world at that particular place.

Exodus 3:5–6 □

When Moses faced the burning bush, in Exodus 3:5–6, he immediately recognised that it was a holy place where God could and should be worshipped. This never became a regular place of worship because the bush was far from Israel; later generations, however, had many similar places where they worshipped God because he had revealed himself there to the leaders of Israel.

The tabernacle and the ark

Exodus 33:7–40:38 □

Exodus 33:7–40:38 records how the Jews who escaped from Egypt worshipped God in a special tent which they erected in the middle of their camp. They called this 'the tent of the Lord's presence' or 'the tabernacle'.

We usually associate the word 'tabernacle' with a *fixed building*, but it is the biblical word for a *moveable tent* which God filled with his presence, with a visible cloud of his glory. When the cloud moved on, God's people picked up the tabernacle and followed the cloud of glory.

The Old Testament contains detailed instructions for the tabernacle's erection and use. A central enclosure marked the holiest part, and this was surrounded by several other enclosures until the boundary of the tabernacle area was reached. The priests' tents were pitched just beyond this, and the people's tents were erected beyond them.

Ezekiel 42:20 □

Ezekiel 42:20 shows that this sort of arrangement was designed to separate that which was holy from that which was not, and to ensure that only those people who were qualified could come into contact with the holiness of God's presence.

The holiest part of the tabernacle, the 'holy of holies', contained 'the ark of the covenant'. This was a gold-covered, wooden box which contained the two tablets of the Law, a pot of manna, and Aaron's rod; we see this in Exodus 25:16, 21; 40:20; Deuteronomy 10:1–5 and Hebrews 9:4–5.

The ark was the place in the tabernacle where God revealed his will – as in Exodus 25:22; 30:36; Leviticus 16:2; Joshua 7:6. The ark was always very closely identified with God's personal presence, for example Numbers 10:35–36; Joshua 4:5, 13.

Nobody knows what happened to either the tabernacle or the ark. The tabernacle is not mentioned after God's people settled in Canaan. The ark, however, is mentioned in Joshua 3:1–5:1; Judges 20:18–28; 1 Samuel 4:1–7; 6:1–23 and 1 Kings 8:1–9. It was installed in the Jerusalem temple by king Solomon, where it resided until Nebuchadnezzar's army ransacked Jerusalem. In New Testament times, the holy of holies in the temple was left empty.

The ark and the tabernacle played an important part in the development of Old Testament worship. They underlined the important truth that God was not tied to one particular place; they showed that God's power and presence could be known only where *Yahweh* chose to reveal himself; and they stressed that God could be worshipped properly only where, and how, he himself chose and directed.

Local sanctuaries

People have always liked to worship near to where they live, and the Old Testament suggests that most Old Testament towns and villages originally had some sort of place for worship – usually an open-air altar where sacrifices could be offered.

Genesis 13:18; 18:1–15; 26:23–26; 28:10–22; 31:43–55; Judges 20:18–28; 1 Samuel 1:1–3:21; 7:16–17; 10:3, 17–27; 11:14–15; 13:8–15; 1 Kings 3:4–15; 5:1–6:37; 12:29–13:32; Amos 3:14; 5:5–6 and 7:16–17 refer to local sanctuaries at Hebron, Beersheba, Mizpah, Bethel, Gilgal, Ramah, Shiloh and Gibeon.

These were part of Israel's religious life before the exodus, but were condemned when they entered Canaan. God wanted his people to worship where *he* chose rather than where *they* chose.

Exodus 25:16–21 ☐
40:20 ☐
Deuteronomy
10:1–5 ☐
Hebrews 9:4–5 ☐
Exodus 25:22 ☐
30:36 ☐
Leviticus 16:2 ☐
Joshua 7:6 ☐
Numbers
10:35–36 ☐
Joshua 4:5 ☐
4:13 ☐
3:1–5:1 ☐
Judges 20:18–28 ☐
1 Samuel 4:1–7 ☐
6:1–23 ☐
1 Kings 8:1–9 ☐
Genesis 13:18 ☐
18:1–15 ☐
26:23–26 ☐
28:10–22 ☐
31:43–55 ☐
Judges 20:18–28 ☐
1 Samuel 1:1–
3:21 ☐
7:16–17 ☐
10:3 ☐
10:17–27 ☐
11:14–15 ☐
13:8–15 ☐
1 Kings 3:4–15 ☐
5:1–6:37 ☐
12:29–
13:32 ☐
Amos 3:14 ☐
5:5–6 ☐
7:16–17 ☐
Deuteronomy
12:5–18 ☐

2 Kings 18:1–8 ☐
      21:3 ☐
      23:1–20 ☐

Jeremiah 2:20 ☐

1 Kings 6:1–7:51 ☐

2 Chronicles
      2:17–5:1 ☐

2 Kings 16:10–18 ☐
      18:1–7 ☐
      21:1–18 ☐

2 Samuel 7:5–7 ☐

Jeremiah 35:1–19 ☐

Isaiah 66:1 ☐

1 Kings 8:27–30 ☐

Psalm 11:4 ☐
      26:8 ☐
      63:1–5 ☐
      84:1–4 ☐
      122:1 ☐

Despite this divine disapproval, the sanctuaries flourished until they were overshadowed by the Jerusalem temple. Its huge staff of priests and musicians ensured its worship was so impressive that people began to ignore the sanctuaries and make pilgrimages to the temple instead.

Sadly, many of the local sanctuaries encouraged the worship of false gods: these were condemned by the prophets and were forcibly closed down. We see this in 2 Kings 18:1–8; 21:3; 23:1–20 and Jeremiah 2:20.

The Jerusalem temple

1 Kings 6:1–7:51 and 2 Chronicles 2:17–5:1 describe the temple's construction. Its general layout was similar to the tabernacle, with a central holy of holies surrounded by other enclosures. Most worship took place in these enclosures, which were often decorated more to reflect the nation's political alliances than to celebrate *Yahweh*. We see this, for example, in 2 Kings 16:10–18; 18:1–7 and 21:1–18.

There was a close connection between the kings and the temple, and 2 Kings 16:18 reveals that a private passage linked the palace to the temple. This means that the temple was more than a place of spiritual worship; it also symbolised the political power of the royal family.

Passages like 2 Samuel 7:5–7; Jeremiah 7:1–27; 35:1–19 and Isaiah 66:1 suggest that the prophets were occasionally unhappy with the temple. At times, like Jesus in Luke 19:45–46, the prophets objected to what was going on in the temple, or they complained that the people were trusting more in the temple than in God. Some of the prophets, however, seem to have believed that covenant faith in *Yahweh* was better served by a simple tent than by a splendid temple.

Despite this, most ordinary Jews were deeply committed to the temple. Even though they knew that *Yahweh* did not literally live in the temple, they still believed that it was the place where they could feel God's presence most directly. We see this, for example, in 1 Kings 8:27–30; Psalm 11:4; 26:8; 63:1–5; 84:1–4 and 122:1.

Local synagogues

The books of Ezra and Nehemiah describe the return of the Jews from exile and the rebuilding of the Jerusalem temple. Worship there, however, was never the same as in the days of the kings, for the effective centre of worship soon shifted to local synagogues.

Synagogue worship differed from temple worship. For example:

- *it was based in local communities and was on a smaller scale*

- *it did not include any ritual sacrifices*

- *its main features were prayer and the reading-and-interpretation of 'the law and the prophets'*

Nobody knows how the synagogues developed, but Ezra's emphasis on reading and interpreting the law seems to have been a key factor. The people's awareness that God had been with them during the exile, that he had accepted their 'temple-less' worship, and that he had brought them back to Israel, underlined the truth that God's presence and power could not be restricted to one place.

God had met with Joseph in a prison cell, Moses by a burning bush, Jonah in a great fish, Jeremiah in a miry well, and Nehemiah in a royal palace, so synagogues developed throughout Israel because the people realised that they could enjoy God's presence just about anywhere.

TYPES OF WORSHIP

We see in *Effective Prayer* and *Salvation by Grace* that prayer and sacrifice were important aspects of Old Testament worship. Jeremiah 6:20 and Amos 4:4 suggest that incense and giving also featured, and the book of Psalms records that singing, dancing, shouting and processions were an integral part of worship. The Old Testament, however, never gives a detailed account of a complete service.

Jeremiah 6:20 ☐

Amos 4:4 ☐

Sacrifice

Passages like Leviticus 1:1–7:38; Numbers 15:1–31 and 28:1–29:40 record the specific instructions for the offering of sacrifices, and we consider these in some detail in *Salvation by Grace*.

Leviticus 1:1–7:38 ☐

Numbers 15:1–31 ☐
28:1–
29:40 ☐

Genesis 4:3–5 and 8:20 show that people worshipped God with sacrifices from the dawn of time, and that God met with them at the time and place of sacrifice. Abraham must have often offered sacrifices or Isaac would not have asked about the lamb in Genesis 22:7.

Genesis 4:3–5 ☐
8:20 ☐
22:7 ☐

Exodus 10:24–26 ☐

Later, the Egyptians endured a series of plagues because Pharaoh would not allow the Israelites to visit the wilderness to worship God with sacrifices. Exodus 10:24–26 reveals two key principles of Old Testament sacrificial worship.

First, people had to allow God to direct their sacrifices; and, second, they could offer only clean animals and birds which actually belonged to them – there had to be some element of genuine, costly self-denial.

Exodus 11–13 ☐

The tenth plague was an act of judgement on Egypt *and* deliverance for Israel. The Passover, in Exodus 11–13, was the beginning not only of Israel's national life, but also of organised regular sacrifices.

After the Passover, while God's people were still wandering in the wilderness, God instructed them about sacrifice. There were to be five principal rituals:

- *the holocaust, or burnt offering*
- *the oblation, or grain offering*
- *the communion, or peace offering*
- *the sin offering*
- *the guilt, reparation or trespass offering*

We can say that:

- *the oblation* and *communion* sacrifices helped the people to express their feelings of being creatures who belonged to God
- *the holocaust* sacrifice represented the people's dedication – and God's acceptance – of everything that they had and were
- *the eating together by priest and people in the communion* sacrifice reminded them of their vital relationship with God
- *the sin* and *guilt* sacrifices enabled the people both to display their human sense of separation from a holy God caused by their sin and guilt, and to cry to God for him to cover it.

In all the sacrifices, only the best would do. We have seen that the worshippers had to sacrifice in a way which depleted their personal resources, but Deuteronomy 23:18 suggests that even this would be unacceptable if the property had been unlawfully acquired.

Deuteronomy 23:18 ☐

The ritual sacrifices were meant to be offered personally and nationally, privately and publicly, regularly and as special needs arose.

Numbers 28–29 list the daily, weekly, monthly and annual public sacrifices; and Exodus 12 shows how the Passover was to be celebrated within the family.

Whenever the people of Israel turned to *Yahweh*, they were supposed to worship him by offering him sacrifices. The Old Testament shows that although the ritual sacrifices were made in different situations for a variety of reasons, the actual act of offering a sacrifice always followed a set pattern. We consider this in detail in *Salvation by Grace*.

Singing and music

The book of Psalms teaches more about the worship of God's people than any other part of the Old Testament, and we consider this in detail in Part Four.

When we look at the Psalms, and at other Old Testament descriptions of worship, we see that singing and music were important elements.

1 Kings 18:27–29 reports that other ancient religions used music to work themselves into a frenzy; 1 Samuel 10:1–13 suggests that a few of God's prophets sometimes used music in the same way; and Amos 5:23 insists that God is not pleased by all spiritual singing and music. Nevertheless, God's people could not properly praise him without joyful singing and music.

Passages like Psalm 22:3 and 63:5 show that it is natural for us to respond to God's holy character in this kind of worship, and the awareness of God's good presence always leads people to worship him with glad songs of praise.

1 Chronicles 15:16–24; 16:4–7 and Ezra 2:41, 70; 3:10–11 refer to special choirs which participated in the worship, and many of the Psalms have a refrain which suggests that one part of the song would be sung by the worshippers and the rest by the choir. We can see this, for example, in Psalms 42, 43 and 46.

2 Samuel 6:5; 1 Chronicles 25:1–5; Psalm 43:4; 68:25; 81:1–3; 98:4–6; 150:3–5 and Isaiah 30:29 show that people played tambourines, harps, lyres, trumpets, rattles, horns, flutes and cymbals in praise of God. Old Testament worship was essentially joyful, and Psalm 42:4 suggests that there was almost a carnival atmosphere during the temple praise.

Numbers 28–29 ☐
Exodus 12 ☐
1 Kings 18:27–29 ☐
1 Samuel 10:1–13 ☐
Amos 5:23 ☐
Psalm 22:3 ☐
63:5 ☐
1 Chronicles 15:16–24 ☐
16:4–7 ☐
Ezra 2:41, 70 ☐
3:10–11 ☐
Psalms 42 ☐
43 ☐
46 ☐
2 Samuel 6:5 ☐
1 Chronicles 25:1–5 ☐
Psalm 43:4 ☐
68:25 ☐
81:1–3 ☐
98:4–6 ☐
150:3–5 ☐
Isaiah 30:29 ☐
Psalm 42:4 ☐

Psalm 26:6 ☐
149:3 ☐
150:4 ☐

2 Samuel 6:1–22 ☐

Psalms 26:6 ☐
42:4 ☐
48:12–14 ☐
68:24–27 ☐
118:19 ☐

Psalms 46:8–10 ☐
48:8 ☐
66:5 ☐

Psalm 26:6 ☐

1 Samuel 1:1–18 ☐

1 Kings 8:22–61 ☐
18:36–37 ☐

Deuteronomy
26:5–10 ☐

1 Samuel 1:26 ☐

1 Kings 8:22, 54 ☐

Psalm 5:7 ☐
51:17 ☐
63:4 ☐

Isaiah 1:15 ☐

Dancing and drama

Some of the Psalms seem to assume dancing, while others actively encourage it – we see this, for example, in Psalm 26:6; 149:3 and 150:4. 2 Samuel 6:1–22 even reports how king David took part in public dancing and was rebuked by his wife for looking foolish.

Psalms 26:6; 42:4; 48:12–14; 68:24–27 and 118:19 describe processions in which the worshippers marched in-and-out of the temple and through the city as an act of praise.

Psalms 46:8–10; 48:8 and 66:5 suggest that God's mighty acts could be re-enacted during the worship to teach about his power; and Psalm 26:6 shows that symbolic actions played a part in worship.

Prayer

The New Testament records that regular times of prayer were held in the temple, but these are not mentioned in the Old Testament; even so, prayer was always a vital part of worship in Israel.

Throughout the Old Testament, it is plain that ordinary people like Hannah could bring their problems to God – as well as prophets and kings. We see this in 1 Samuel 1:1–18; 1 Kings 8:22–61 and 18:36–37.

Deuteronomy 26:5–10 shows that 'the Law' contained prayers to be used on special occasions, and the book of Psalms contains many prayers which were used by individuals and groups of worshippers.

1 Samuel 1:26; 1 Kings 8:22, 54; Psalm 5:7; 51:17; 63:4 and Isaiah 1:15 show that many different bodily positions were used in prayer; but the inner attitude was always more important than the outer posture.

TIMES FOR WORSHIP

Old Testament worship involved the way that the people lived as well as what they did at the holy places. God was available to all his people at every time and in every place, and so the local sanctuaries, tabernacle and temple, were always open for people to use them in worship.

There were, however, regular special times when people stopped work to join together and celebrate God's grace and goodness.

The Sabbath

The Hebrew word *sabbat* means 'cessation' or 'rest', and Genesis 2:2; Exodus 20:11 and 31:17 state that God 'rested' from his work of creation and was 'refreshed'.

Genesis 2:2 ☐
Exodus 20:11 ☐
31:17 ☐

The Old Testament Sabbath principle of desisting from work for one day a week is based on God's personal example of sabbath rest. Of course, God was not a tired worker who needed to rest; nevertheless, his action set humanity an important example to follow. Exodus 23:12 and 34:21 show that the Sabbath began as a day of rest when everyone – including slaves and foreigners – could renew themselves for work.

Exodus 23:12 ☐
34:21 ☐

It seems that worship was part of this Sabbath renewing process. Passages like Leviticus 19:30; Numbers 28:9–10; 2 Kings 11:5–8 Isaiah 1:13; 2:11; Jeremiah 17:21–22 and Amos 8:5 describe what happened on the Sabbath, and show that the activities did not always please God.

Leviticus 19:30 ☐
Numbers 28:9–10 ☐
2 Kings 11:5–8 ☐
Isaiah 1:13 ☐
2:11 ☐
Jeremiah
17:21–22 ☐
Amos 8:5 ☐

For Jews, the Sabbath was a day to reflect on their national roots, to celebrate God's greatness, and to renew their commitment to the covenant faith. This is why the law, Exodus 20:8–11, orders God's people to observe the Sabbath and dedicate the whole day to *Yahweh*.

Exodus 20:8–11 ☐
31:12–17 ☐

Exodus 31:12–17 and Deuteronomy 5:13–15 set out the biblical teaching on the Sabbath, and Isaiah 58:13–14 shows that it was meant to be a day of joyful celebration.

Deuteronomy
5:13–15 ☐
Isaiah 58:13–14 ☐

The Passover

God's people continually looked back to their deliverance from slavery in Egypt. They marked this with an annual festival that they held in their homes: this celebrated the way that God's covenant relationship with them had been evidenced in the events of the exodus.

At first, a lamb was sacrificed in each family home and the feast was celebrated entirely privately. Later, however, the lambs were sacrificed in the temple with all the splendour of a great spiritual occasion, and were then eaten at home in family celebrations – this stressed the link between the *national* and *family* elements of the exodus deliverance.

Deuteronomy
16:5–6 ☐

Numbers 9:1–4 ☐

Deuteronomy
        16:1–8 ☐

2 Kings 23:21–22 ☐

2 Chronicles
        30:1–27 ☐
        35:1–19 ☐

Leviticus 23:9–14 ☐

Numbers
        28:16–25 ☐

Numbers
        28:26–31 ☐

Leviticus
        23:15–21 ☐

Deuteronomy
        16:12 ☐

Exodus 24:7 ☐

Leviticus
        23:33–44 ☐

Deuteronomy
        16:13–17 ☐
        27:9–10 ☐
        31:9–13 ☐

Joshua 24:1–28 ☐

Nehemiah
        8:13–18 ☐

This festival was considered to be so important there was a special provision that anyone who missed the Passover because they were ritually unclean could celebrate it a month after the proper date. Passages like Numbers 9:1–4; Deuteronomy 16:1–8; 2 Kings 23:21–22; 2 Chronicles 30:1–27 and 35:1–19 illustrate the place of the Passover in Old Testament worship.

Harvest festivals

The Old Testament mentions three major festivals which seem to have related to the agricultural year. The Scriptures link them, however, more to the great events of Israel's history than to the cycle of seasons.

- *unleavened bread* was related to the barley harvest, but was celebrated at the same time of year as the Passover. This meant that the two festivals were closely connected and together commemorated the escape from Egypt. We see this in Leviticus 23:9–14 and Numbers 28:16–25.

- *weeks* or *pentecost* celebrated the end of the wheat harvest, and special offerings were made at all the sanctuaries. In time, this became the festival when God's people celebrated the giving of the law at Mount Sinai. We see this in Numbers 28:26–31; Leviticus 23:15–21 and Deuteronomy 16:12.

- *shelters* or *tabernacles* came at the end of the growing season and celebrated the fruit harvest. It was an especially joyful festival, and the worshippers lived in flimsy shelters for seven days – partly because this was what the farmers did to protect their crops, but mainly to remember their ancestors' journey through the wilderness when they slept in rough tents.

This festival celebrated Israel's covenant faith, and many scholars believe that it included a moment when the people dedicated themselves again to the demands of God's law and covenant. We see this in Exodus 24:7; Leviticus 23:33–44; Deuteronomy 16:13–17; 27:9–10; 31:9–13; Joshua 24:1–28; Nehemiah 8:13–18.

Other festivals

Each year, God's people also celebrated three other important festivals which were not related to the agricultural year.

- *trumpets* – the day of trumpets is mentioned in Numbers 29:1 and Leviticus 23:24. It was called 'a memorial of blowing trumpets' and 'a sabbath'. On this day, God's people rested from work, worshipped him with sacrifices, and celebrated their nationhood.

  Numbers 29:1 ☐

  Leviticus 23:24 ☐

- *purim* – this feast was a later addition to the Jewish religious year, and is described in Esther 9. It was established by Mordecai to commemorate the Jews' remarkable deliverance from Haman's plots, and it was a day of feasting, rejoicing and practical jokes.

  Esther 9 ☐

- *atonement* – the day of atonement is described in Leviticus 16. It was an annual national sacrifice for sin – in contrast to the regular *personal* sacrifices for sin. It was the most important day in the Jewish year, and the only occasion when 'the holy of holies' was entered, and then only by the high priest.

  Leviticus 16 ☐

  The high priest took two goats to atone for all the sins of all the people of Israel. He slaughtered one goat, and sprinkled its blood on the altar. He placed his hands on the other goat, confessed all the wickedness and rebellion of God's people, and drove the goat away into the desert so that it would symbolically 'bear' their sins away. We consider the feast fully in *Salvation by Grace*.

Varied worship

We have seen that Old Testament worship was a very varied experience, but it did not include preaching.

Nehemiah 8:7–9 shows that the law was expounded during worship after the return from exile, but the main emphasis in earlier days was always on praise and celebration.

Nehemiah 8:7–9 ☐

Worship was the people's response to God as he had made himself known through the events of history and in their everyday experience. As they went to the sanctuaries, they were reminded of God's past goodness and so were given fresh hope for their lives. They were, however, also challenged by God's holiness, as they faced their need of repentance and forgiveness, and they offered sacrifices to secure this.

As time passed by, the repetitive nature of much Old Testament worship led the prophets to question its effectiveness, and to see it as merely one stage on the road to a closer and deeper covenant relationship with God.

PROPHETS, PRIESTS AND KINGS

2 Samuel 6:17 ☐
24:25 ☐
1 Kings 5:1–6:14 ☐
12:26–33 ☐
Amos 7:13 ☐
1 Kings 15:11–15 ☐
2 Kings 1:1–19 ☐
16:1–18 ☐
18:1–7 ☐
21:1–9 ☐
22:3–
23:23 ☐
1 Samuel 13:8–10 ☐
14:35 ☐
2 Samuel 6:1–19 ☐
24:25 ☐
1 Kings 3:3–4 ☐
8:14–66 ☐
12:32–
13:1 ☐
2 Kings 16:1–16 ☐
19:14–19 ☐
Judges 17:1–13 ☐
1 Samuel 1–3:21 ☐
Amos 7:10–13 ☐
1 Samuel 9:3–16 ☐
Leviticus 10:8–11 ☐
13:1–8 ☐
Ezekiel 22:26 ☐
44:23 ☐
Haggai 2:11–14 ☐
Leviticus 1:1–7:38 ☐
Numbers 15:1–31 ☐
28:1–
29:40 ☐
Joshua 3:6–17 ☐
4:9–11 ☐
Numbers 6:22–26 ☐
1 Samuel 1:17 ☐

The Old Testament system of formal worship needed some full-time officials to look after the places of worship and to supervise what went on. The Scriptures often refer to gatekeepers, musicians and other skilled workers who served in the temple; but the kings, priests and prophets were the key figures in Israel's worship.

Kings

Throughout the whole history of Israel and Judah, the kings played an important part in public worship. For example, the kings:

- *established centres of worship* – 2 Samuel 6:17; 24:25; 1 Kings 5:1–6:14; 12:26–33; Amos 7:13

- *took charge of religious policy making* – 1 Kings 15:11–15; 2 Kings 1:1–19; 16:1–18; 18:1–7; 21:1–9; 22:3–23:23

- *conducted worship* – 1 Samuel 13:8–10; 14:35; 2 Samuel 6:1–19; 24:25; 1 Kings 3:3–4; 8:14–66; 12:32–13:1; 2 Kings 16:1–16; 19:14–19

Priests

After the exile and the end of the monarchy, the priests became political leaders, but their spiritual functions were still the most important part of their work. The Bible shows that the priests:

- *cared for the sanctuaries throughout the land* – Judges 17:1–13; 1 Samuel 1–3:21; Amos 7:10–13

- *gave advice when consulted* – 1 Samuel 9:3–16

- *gave instructions about worship* – Leviticus 10:8–11; 13:1–8; Ezekiel 22:26; 44:23; Haggai 2:11–14

- *officiated at sacrifices and poured the sacrificial blood on the altar* – Leviticus 1:1–7:38; Numbers 15:1–31 and 28:1–29:40

- *were the custodians of the ark and the law* – Joshua 3:6–17; 4:9–11

- *mediated between God and the people* – Numbers 6:22–26; 1 Samuel 1:17

It was this function as mediator which was most characteristic of the priestly role. Because the priests were specially consecrated to God, they could deal with the holiness of a place of worship. Through the priest's mediation, God and people were brought together in a tangible way at worship.

The priests were the only ones who ministered exclusively to God. Exodus 19:4–6 shows that God's ultimate purpose was to have a whole nation of priests who existed for the praise of his glory. This ministry was foreshadowed through the calling of the priests to serve continually in the sanctuary.

Exodus 19:4–6 ☐

When the priests functioned properly in the temple and tabernacle, the glory of God was revealed and the holy presence of God was manifest in the sanctuary. We see this, for example, in Exodus 40:34–35 and 2 Chronicles 5:13–14.

Exodus 40:34–35 ☐

2 Chronicles
5:13–14 ☐

The priests were called to the presence of God, and this still remains the goal of all true worship. When the priests offered God the worship that he sought, the whole nation knew the manifestation and blessing of God. As we see in *Glory in the Church*, we have this function today. But, whereas the priestly office was reserved for one tribe and family in the Old Covenant, it is now the calling of all believers in the church.

The glory of the Lord, and the blessings of his presence, flow as we fulfil our priestly function of offering continuous praise and worship to Almighty God.

Prophets

Some modern believers seem to think that the priests and prophets were opposed to each other, that the priests were concerned only with pointless ritual, and that the prophets brought the life-giving message of God. But Jeremiah 18:18 shows that the priests and prophets were complementary.

Jeremiah 18:18 ☐

Isaiah 1:10–17 ☐

Amos 5:21–24 ☐

Hosea 6:6 ☐

Micah 6:6–8 ☐

Jeremiah 5:31 ☐
23:11 ☐
26:7–16 ☐
29:26 ☐

While it is true that some prophets criticised dead formality – as in Isaiah 1:10–17; Amos 5:21–24; Hosea 6:6 and Micah 6:6–8 – they were also involved with the organised worship of the nation. For example:

- *priests and prophets worked alongside each other* – Jeremiah 5:31; 23:11; 26:7, 16; 29:26; Lamentations 2:20; Zechariah 7:1–3

Lamentations
2:20 ☐

Zechariah 7:1–3 ☐

- *some prophets had a room in the temple* – Jeremiah 35:3–4

Jeremiah 35:3–4 ☐

Jeremiah 1:1 ☐

Ezekiel 1:1 ☐

Psalm 12:5 ☐

    81:5–16 ☐

    85:9–13 ☐

    91:14–16 ☐

2 Chronicles

    34:30 ☐

2 Kings 23:2 ☐

1 Chronicles

    25:1–6 ☐

2 Chronicles

    20:13–19 ☐

- *the prophets often delivered their messages in the context of organised worship, and often related them to the main festivals*

- *some prophets were members of priestly families* – Jeremiah 1:1; Ezekiel 1:1

- *some Psalms imply that someone spoke in the name of God during the liturgy of worship and others contain messages which came directly from God* – Psalm 12:5; 81:5–16; 85:9–13; 91:14–16

It is interesting to note that the people who are identified as 'levites' by the writer of 2 Chronicles 34:30 are the same people who are called prophets by the writer of 2 Kings 23:2. In both 1 and 2 Chronicles, these 'levites' are often given expressly prophetic functions, including the utterance of messages on God's behalf during worship – we see this, for example, in 1 Chronicles 25:1–6 and 2 Chronicles 20:13–19.

People

Most worshippers were not prophets, priests or kings, they were simple working men and women in the small towns and villages of Israel. Most of the Old Testament tells us little about the precise details of their worship; one book, however, stands out, and is fundamental to our understanding of the worship of ordinary people – and to our worship today.

The book of Psalms seems to be a detailed account of the worshipping activities at the Jerusalem temple in the period of the kings just before the exile to Babylon. This long Old Testament book is so basic to biblical worship in spirit and truth, that we now move on to consider it in more detail.

PART FOUR

worship in the psalms

The Old Testament book of Psalms contains 150 pieces of spiritual poetry which are arranged in five collections or 'mini-books' – 1–41; 42–72; 73–89; 90–106; 107–150.

The end of each of these five collections (for example, 41:13) is marked by a 'doxology', by a formal phrase of praise to God. Psalm 150 seems to be a doxology to the complete book of Psalms.

Most scholars think that the Psalms were assembled into these five books so that they could be used in the worship of the restored temple – which was built in Jerusalem by Nehemiah after the return from exile.

Psalms like 137 and 126 must have been written at that time, but most of the other Psalms would have been written long before the exile, during the time of the kings. This means that they show us how the people of Israel were worshipping their God one thousand years before Christ was born.

The five collections must have been selected from earlier and separate collections – perhaps from 'hymnbooks' by Asaph (50, 73–83), Korah (42, 49, 84–85, 87–88) and David (3–41, 51–72), and from

Psalm 41:13 ☐
Psalm 150 ☐

Psalm 137 ☐
126 ☐

'songsheets' for special occasions like the annual pilgrimage to Jerusalem (120–134) and the family Passover meal (105–107, 111–118, 135–136, 146–150).

The fact that some Psalms duplicate each other seems to prove that there must have been several earlier parallel collections, for example 14 and 53, 40:13–17 and 70, 108 and 57:7–11 and 60:5–12.

Psalm 14 ☐
53 ☐
40:13–17 ☐
70 ☐
108 ☐
57:7–11 ☐
60:5–12 ☐

We consider the great importance of understanding God's name in *Knowing the Father*. This is particularly important in the Psalms, for they reveal more detail about God's name and nature than any other part of the Bible. In fact, it seems that the five scriptural collections of Psalms were probably constructed around God's name: for example, books one, four and five focus almost entirely on worshipping *Yahweh*, whereas books two and three concentrate on worshipping *Elohim*.

TITLES OF PSALMS

In most English Bibles, nearly all the Psalms seem to have a title. Although these titles were not part of the original scriptural Psalms, they do preserve traditional Jewish ideas about the Psalms.

Some titles contain musical directions; for example, *Michtam* in 56–58 probably means 'sing in a quiet voice'. Other titles stipulate the tune to be used; for example, 56 'the silent dove in distant lands', 57 'do not destroy', 60 'lily of the testimony'. And a few titles prescribe the particular instruments which must be played; for example, 4, 5, 6.

Psalm 56 ☐
57 ☐
60 ☐
4 ☐
5 ☐
6 ☐
88 ☐
89 ☐
90 ☐
145 ☐
100 ☐
89 ☐
90 ☐
45 ☐
50 ☐
51 ☐

Some titles link the Psalm with a specific person; for example, 88 Heman, 89 Ethan, 90 Moses. Other titles identify the type of Psalm; for example, 145 praise, 100 thanksgiving, 89 contemplation, 90 prayer, 45 love song, and so on. Still more titles relate the Psalm to a specific event; for example, 50, 51, 54, 56, 57.

Psalms of David

We do not know what some of the traditional titles mean. For example, the phrase 'a Psalm of David' (which appears in the title of seventy three Psalms) could sometimes mean that it was written for

David, could other times mean that it was written by David, and could occasionally mean that it was part of a collection issued by the palace.

1 Samuel 16:16–23 records that David was a gifted musician and poet, and 1 Chronicles 25:1–8 shows his great interest in prophetic music, so it is surely likely that he wrote many of the Psalms which are traditionally accredited to him. Indeed, Psalm 18 is simply an edited version of his poem in 2 Samuel 22. Several Psalms are closely linked to particular events in David's life and seem to express his personal feelings and responses to God, for example:

- Psalm 59 *with* 1 Samuel 19:11–24

- Psalm 34 *with* 1 Samuel 21

- Psalms 57 and 142 *with* 1 Samuel 22:1–5; 24:3–15

- Psalm 52 *with* 1 Samuel 22

- Psalm 54 *with* 1 Samuel 23:19–29

- Psalm 63 *with* 1 Samuel 24:1–2, 22; 2 Samuel 15:13–37

- Psalm 60 *with* 2 Samuel 8:13

- Psalms 32 and 51 *with* 2 Samuel 11–12

- Psalm 3 *with* 2 Samuel 15:13–37

- Psalm 18 *with* 2 Samuel 22

TYPES OF PSALMS

The Psalms seem to express the whole range of our human feelings and experiences, from deep depression to ecstatic joy.

Some Psalms (like 145–150) are wonderful hymns of praise to God, and are songs which can be used by worshippers who are at peace with God and the world. Other Psalms, however, reflect the dark and painful moments of human experience.

Some (like 51 and 130) are for worshippers who recognise that their personal guilt is the cause of their problem. While others (like 13 and 71) are for worshippers who think that they are innocent and should not be suffering at all.

1 Samuel
    16:16–23 ☐
1 Chronicles
    25:1–8 ☐
Psalm 18 ☐
2 Samuel 22 ☐
Psalm 59 ☐
1 Samuel
    19:11–24 ☐
Psalm 34 ☐
1 Samuel 21 ☐
Psalms 57 ☐
    142 ☐
1 Samuel 22:1–5 ☐
    24:3–15 ☐
Psalm 52 ☐
1 Samuel 22 ☐
Psalm 54 ☐
1 Samuel
    23:19–29 ☐
Psalm 63 ☐
1 Samuel 24:1–2 ☐
2 Samuel
    15:13–37 ☐
Psalm 60 ☐
2 Samuel 8:13 ☐
Psalms 32 ☐
    51 ☐
2 Samuel 11–12 ☐
Psalm 3 ☐
2 Samuel
    15:13–37 ☐
Psalm 18 ☐
2 Samuel 22 ☐
Psalm 145 ☐
    146 ☐
    147 ☐
    148 ☐
    149 ☐
    150 ☐
    51 ☐
    130 ☐
    13 ☐
    71 ☐

Psalm 44 ☐
74 ☐
80 ☐
83 ☐
45 ☐
30 ☐
92 ☐
116 ☐

Many Psalms (like 44, 74, 80, 83) enable the whole nation to respond together to God in a time of national uncertainty or disaster. A few (like 45) help people to celebrate together in a great event like a coronation or a royal wedding. While others (like 30, 92, 116) are songs which enable individuals to express their gratitude to God when they have been delivered from a personal trial.

There are Psalms which plead with God and Psalms which praise him. There are appeals for forgiveness and appeals for the destruction of enemies; prayers for the king and prayers for the nation. There are Psalms which probe life's problems and Psalms which celebrate the greatness of God's law. Many Psalms are a mixture of several themes, but they were all part of the worshipping life of God's people.

Hebrew poems

If we are to understand the book of Psalms correctly, and to use it helpfully in worship today, we must appreciate that it is a collection of inspired Hebrew poems which was meant to be used in worship. The Psalms are not sermons to be read, nor doctrinal treatises to be discussed; they are songs to be sung. In fact, most scholars consider the book to be the five-volume hymnbook of the second temple.

Judges 5:30 ☐

Many people today think that poetry is rather remote and intellectual. Hebrew poetry, however, was much closer to modern oratory than modern poetry. For example, Judges 5:30 uses *reiteration* to make the passage memorable and impressive in much the same way as Winston Churchill used it in his classic wartime speeches.

Numbers 23:19 ☐

Hebrew poetry differs from ours essentially by using *parallelism* – the echoing of the thought of one line in a second line which is its partner; for example, Numbers 23:19. This device somehow communicates great dignity and creates an impression of spaciousness which allows time for the thought to impact on the listener. It also enables the poet to present more than one facet of a matter, as in Isaiah 55:8.

Isaiah 55:8 ☐

Psalm 119 ☐
34 ☐
111 ☐
112 ☐
145 ☐

Some aspects of Hebrew poetry are completely lost in translation. Psalm 119, for example, is an alphabetical poem with 22 equal length sections (eight modern verses) which each begin with one of the 22 letters in the Hebrew alphabet – Psalms 34, 111, 112 and 145 use the same device.

Parallelism, and the use of a *refrain* (as in 46 and 136), survive translation into any language, and are used throughout the Psalms to provide us with poetic words for worship which are as powerful, relevant and memorable today as they were three thousand years ago when they were first written in praise of God.

Psalm 46 ☐
136 ☐

Hymns of praise

Although we can say that every Psalm is a poem for worship, there are three general forms of poem – *hymns*, *lamentations* and *thanksgivings*.

Psalms 8, 19, 29, 33, 46–48, 76, 84, 87, 93, 96–100, 103–106, 113–114, 117, 122, 135–136 and 145–150 are straightforward hymns of praise, much the same as the hymns we still sing today.

Typically, Psalms which are hymns begin with an invitation to praise God. The body of the hymn then suggests some motives for praise, and describes some of the wonders of God in creation and/or history (especially in his saving work for his people). A hymn normally ends by repeating the opening invitation or by closing with a brief prayer.

Some hymns (for example, 46, 48, 76, 84, 87, 122) focus on the glories of the holy city, Zion or Jerusalem, and present it prophetically as both the dwelling place of God *and* the goal of pilgrimage. Other hymns (for example, 47, 93, 96–98) use prophetic language to celebrate the universal sovereignty and absolute kingship of God.

Psalms 8 ☐
19 ☐
29 ☐
33 ☐
48 ☐
76 ☐
84 ☐
87 ☐
122 ☐
47 ☐
93 ☐
96 ☐
97 ☐
98 ☐

Laments about suffering

A whole group of Psalms address God directly, rather than describing and acclaiming his glories.

Typically, these poetic laments begin by invoking God; they then add either an appeal for help, a prayer, or an expression of confidence in God. The main body of the Psalm usually describes the worshipper's misfortunes in images which were relevant to that day – for example, waters of the abyss, snares of death, savage beasts, broken bones, wildly beating heart, and so on.

Some of these laments (like 7, 12, 26) contain protestations of innocence, or complaints about God's seeming absence or forgetfulness (like 9–10, 22, 44). Others express confidence in the midst of problems (like 3, 5, 42–43, 55–57, 63, 130).

Psalm 7 ☐
12 ☐
26 ☐
9 ☐
10 ☐
22 ☐
44 ☐
3 ☐
5 ☐
42 ☐
43 ☐
55 ☐
56 ☐
57 ☐
63 ☐
130 ☐

Psalm 4 ☐
11 ☐
16 ☐
23 ☐
62 ☐
121 ☐
125 ☐
131 ☐
6 ☐
69 ☐
140 ☐
12 ☐
60 ☐
74 ☐
13 ☐
17 ☐

A few laments are composed of one long appeal to God – for example, 4, 11, 16, 23, 62, 121, 125, 131. Many end with an acknowledgement that the appeal has been heard, and with a thanksgiving for God's answer (as in 6, 22, 69 140).

Some lamentations essentially express *corporate* despair at a national catastrophe (like 12, 44, 60, 74, 79, 80, 83, 85, 106, 123, 129, 137) and plead with God to save and restore his people.

Most, however, express *individual* despair about the problems of death, persecution, exile, old age, sickness, slander, and so on. Psalms like 3, 5–7, 13, 17, 22, 25, 26, 28, 31, 35, 38, 42–43, 51, 54–57, 59, 63–64, 69–71, 77, 86, 102, 120, 130 and 140–143 were written to express individual needs – even though they were often sung corporately.

Songs of thanksgiving

Psalm 18 ☐
21 ☐
30 ☐
33 ☐
34 ☐
40 ☐
65 ☐
92 ☐
116 ☐
118 ☐
124 ☐
129 ☐
138 ☐
144 ☐
89 ☐
119 ☐
27 ☐
28 ☐

Although some lamentations end with gratitude to God, several Psalms have thanksgiving as their main theme – for example, 18, 21, 30, 33, 34, 40, 65–68, 92, 116, 118, 124, 129, 138 and 144.

Again, some of these Psalms express *corporate* thanksgiving for a successful harvest or a national danger which has been averted, while others express *individual* thanksgiving for God's personal answer.

These not strict divisions, for some Psalms move from one form to another. For example, 89 begins as a hymn of praise, passes into a long prophetic poem, and ends with a lament; 119 is both a hymn of praise to the law and an individual lament; and some laments are preceded by a prayer (27 and 31) or followed by a thanksgiving (28 and 57).

PROPHETIC PSALMS

Psalm 2 ☐
50 ☐
75 ☐
81 ☐
82 ☐
85 ☐
95 ☐
100 ☐

1 Chronicles 25:1–3 shows that prophetic music, prophetic praise, prophetic thanksgiving and prophetic psalmists were an integral part of worship during the reign of king David.

Some Psalms include prophetic sayings, while others are expanded prophecies put to music – for example, 2, 50, 75, 81–82, 85, 95 and 110.

It seems likely that these were prophecies which were delivered in the course of a temple service by a prophet, and were then used regularly in worship.

The Psalms which are hymns of praise about the holy city and the kingship of God are obviously prophetic, for they look forward to a time of future renewal – to what came to be called 'the messianic age'.

The most important prophetic Psalms, however, are the 'royal Psalms' which are scattered through all five books. These include:

- *pronouncements addressed to the king* – 2, 110

- *prayers for the king* – 20, 61, 72

- *thanksgivings for the king* – 21

- *prayers of the king* – 18, 28, 63, 101

- *a royal processional song* – 132

- *a hymn of the king* – 144

- *a royal wedding song* – 45

Psalm 2 ☐
110 ☐
20 ☐
61 ☐
72 ☐
21 ☐
18 ☐
28 ☐
63 ☐
101 ☐
132 ☐
144 ☐
45 ☐

At one level, these Psalms simply concern a particular king of Israel or Judah from the time of the kings, and Psalms 2, 72 and 110 could even have been composed as hymns to be sung at a coronation. But they also point beyond the king of that day, for they claim that he is a son of God, that his reign is endless and stretches to the ends of the earth, that he will establish permanent peace and justice, and that he will be the saviour of his people.

The regular singing of these songs kept the hope alive that the promises made to David would be fulfilled – we consider these in *Salvation by Grace* and *Knowing the Son*. The fact that they were still sung long after the end of the monarchy shows that Israel was looking forward to a king, to the *Messiah*, who would fulfil these prophecies.

The *Messiah* is not mentioned by name in any of the Psalms, but the Jews believed that he was foreshadowed in these Psalms. And the New Testament writers were convinced that these Psalms applied to Jesus as the long-prophesied *Messiah*.

Psalms like 2, 72 and 110 present an ideal king/priest/judge who was never fully realised in any actual king of Israel or Judah. Only the *Messiah* combines these roles in the endless, universal reign of peace and justice prophesied in the poetry.

Psalm 22 ☐
Matthew 27:46 ☐
John 20:25 ☐
Mark 15:24 ☐
Psalm 69:21 ☐
Matthew 27:34,48 ☐
Psalm 2:7 ☐
Acts 13:33 ☐
Psalm 8:6 ☐
Hebrews 2:6–10 ☐
Psalm 16:10 ☐
Acts 2:27 ☐
　　13:35 ☐
Psalm 22:8 ☐
Matthew 27:43 ☐
Psalm 40:7–8 ☐
Hebrews 10:7 ☐
Psalm 41:9 ☐
John 13:18 ☐
Psalm 45:6 ☐
Hebrews 1:8 ☐
Psalm 69:9 ☐
John 2:17 ☐
Psalm 110:4 ☐
Hebrews 7:17 ☐
Psalm 118:22 ☐
Matthew 21:42 ☐
Psalm 118:26 ☐
Matthew 21:9 ☐
Psalm 8 ☐
　　16 ☐
　　22 ☐
　　35 ☐
　　40 ☐
　　41 ☐
　　68 ☐
　　69 ☐
　　97 ☐
　　102 ☐
　　118 ☐
　　119 ☐
Psalm 139 ☐

Other prophetic Psalms depict human suffering in terms which seem exaggerated in relation to ordinary experience, but which proved to be extraordinarily accurate descriptions of the actual sufferings of Christ.

Under God's inspiration, the prophetic poets chose words which were full of great significance. Psalm 22, which Jesus quoted on the cross in Matthew 27:46, is the most striking example: verse 16 can be clearly seen in John 20:25 and verse 18 in Mark 15:24. Psalm 69:21 is another example, and this points forward to Matthew 27:34, 48.

The New Testament insists that many Psalms point prophetically to Jesus, for example:

- Psalm 2:7 – Acts 13:33
- Psalm 8:6 – Hebrews 2:6–10
- Psalm 16:10 – Acts 2:27; 13:35
- Psalm 22:8 – Matthew 27:43
- Psalm 40:7–8 – Hebrews 10:7
- Psalm 41:9 – John 13:18
- Psalm 45:6 – Hebrews 1:8
- Psalm 69:9 – John 2:17
- Psalm 110:4 – Hebrews 7:17
- Psalm 118:22 – Matthew 21:42
- Psalm 118:26 – Matthew 21:9

Some scholars believe that many more Psalms than just the 'royal' Psalms point to Jesus. For example, they argue that 8, 16, 22, 35, 40, 41, 68, 69, 97, 102, 118 and 119 anticipate Christ in some way; and they maintain that all the Psalms about the holy city and the kingship of God apply to Christ's mind and mission.

PROBLEM AREAS

Many believers rejoice in large parts of the Psalms but recoil from other parts. For example, in Psalm 139, they appreciate verses 1–18 and verses 23–24, but are appalled by verses 19–22.

There seem to be two special problems in the Psalms.

- *self-justification*

- *the tendency to call down a terrible vengeance*

We cannot ignore the difficult sections, for they are part of God's Word and are alongside passages which nobody would question. And we cannot explain them away simply by saying that the writers did not know about Jesus. They possessed God's law; they knew that nobody was perfect by God's standards; they knew that they were meant to behave in a loving way to others, even to their enemies; and they knew that the law set strict limits on retaliation.

Self justification

We need to appreciate that the writers of the Psalms made *comparative* claims to righteousness, not *absolute* claims: they compared themselves with the people around them rather than with God. In doing this, they recognised the essential difference between people who try to do God's law and will, and those who ignore God's law and will.

The writers, however, were well aware of their personal sin when they did compare themselves to God's standards: we see this supremely in the seven 'penitential' Psalms – 6, 32, 38, 51, 102, 130 and 143. Deep repentance exists alongside self-justification in the Psalms as much as it exists in those modern believers who gaze at the world in horror and at God in awe.

Psalm 6 ☐
32 ☐
38 ☐
51 ☐
102 ☐
130 ☐
143 ☐

We also need to appreciate that the writers were often presenting themselves as 'indignant plaintiffs' who were putting their case before God as judge. Their tone may jar in our modern ears, but their point-of-view is right.

Vengeance

Several Psalms curse the wicked and call for vengeance upon them, and some believers respond to this by condemning these Psalms as utterly 'un-Christian'. We need to recognise, however, that the writers knew God as a perfectly holy being who could not look at evil and could not tolerate any wrongdoing. Their pleas for vengeance were based in their understanding of God's name and character: they rightly thought that his nature demanded an active, punitive response to sin.

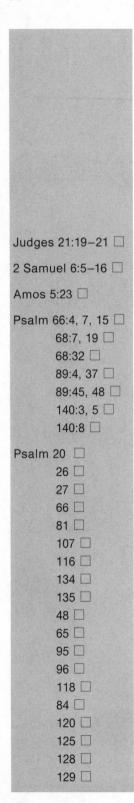

Judges 21:19–21 ☐

2 Samuel 6:5–16 ☐

Amos 5:23 ☐

Psalm 66:4, 7, 15 ☐

68:7, 19 ☐

68:32 ☐

89:4, 37 ☐

89:45, 48 ☐

140:3, 5 ☐

140:8 ☐

Psalm 20 ☐

26 ☐

27 ☐

66 ☐

81 ☐

107 ☐

116 ☐

134 ☐

135 ☐

48 ☐

65 ☐

95 ☐

96 ☐

118 ☐

84 ☐

120 ☐

125 ☐

128 ☐

129 ☐

The writers did not want God to smite the wicked because the wicked had annoyed them; they wanted God to smite them because they knew that he had to act self-consistently with his holiness – we consider this fully *in Knowing the Father* and *Salvation by Grace*.

We also need to recognise that the writers were realistic in acknowledging that right cannot triumph without the actual over-throw of evil and the active punishment of wrong. If we are comfortable praying 'Your kingdom come', we should not be uncomfortable singing a Psalm which spells out what this means in practice! Very many of these so-called 'difficult' passages merely prophetically foreshadow the book of Revelation.

WORSHIP AND THE PSALMS

We have seen that the book of Psalms is the Old Testament hymn-book. It is filled with the spiritual songs which God's people used in praise, worship and thanksgiving for over a thousand years.

All the great festivals of *Yahweh* were celebrated with singing and dancing, as in Judges 21:19–21 and 2 Samuel 6:5–16, and Amos 5:23 records that even sacrifices were offered with singing.

We have seen that many of the Psalms have musical or liturgical instructions in the titles, and the mysterious word *selah* obviously directed the way that the Psalm was used in public worship.

Nobody knows what *selah* means in, for example, Psalm 66:4, 7, 15; 68:7, 19, 32; 89:4, 37, 45, 48 and 140:3, 5, 8. Some argue that it prompted the congregation to sing louder, while others maintain that it directed them to stop singing for a moment while the musicians played 'theme' music.

Psalms 20, 26, 27, 66, 81, 107, 116, 134 and 135 plainly refer to public worship. It is clear that these Psalms – and 48, 65, 95, 96 and 118 – were sung in the temple courtyards, and that 84, 120–134 could easily have been sung by worshippers on their journey to the temple meetings.

Some Psalms (like 125, 128 and 129) have clearly been adapted for public worship by the addition of blessings, while other Psalms are designated for use on particular occasions – for example, 92 on the Sabbath and 30 at the feast of dedication.

Psalm 92 ☐
30 ☐

The value of the Psalms

The Psalms were the basic worship 'tool' of God's Old Testament people. God inspired people to write words which helped his children to approach him whatever their situation.

The Psalms were also sung and used by Jesus, by his disciples, by Paul, the apostles and the members of the early church. Some of the great New testament songs of praise are modelled on the Psalms – as in Luke 1:46–55, 68–79 and 2:29–32.

Luke 1:46–55 ☐
1:68–79 ☐
2:29–32 ☐

The Psalms inspired the apostles when they were persecuted and were an integral part of their message – we see this, for example, in Acts 2: 25–28; 4:25–26 and 13:33. And the early church used the Psalms to set out their key beliefs about Jesus – as in Hebrews 1:6, 10–13; 2:6–8; 5:6; 10:5–7.

Acts 2:25–28 ☐
4:25–26 ☐
13:33 ☐

Hebrews 1:6 ☐
1:10–13 ☐
2:6–8 ☐
5:6 ☐
10:5–7 ☐

Throughout the ages, Christians have adopted the Psalms, interpreted them in the light of the cross, and used them in public and private worship. In most Christian traditions today, at least one Psalm is read or sung in public worship at every service.

Somehow, these 3,000-year-old songs of praise, lament and thanksgiving, seem to be universally relevant, for they express the attitude that all worshippers should all have towards God.

But the Psalms have an even deeper meaning for Christian believers, for we can now use them to praise and thank God for revealing himself fully in Jesus, for redeeming us in Christ, and for anointing us with his Spirit. The hopes which were first sung in the services of Israel have been fulfilled, for the *Messiah* has come, he does reign, and we are summoned to worship him.

PART FIVE

worship in the new testament

All four Gospels show that Jesus and his disciples continued the pattern of Old Testament worship by observing the Sabbath, celebrating the festivals, singing the Psalms, and worshipping at the Jerusalem temple and the local synagogues.

Matthew 4:23; 9:35 and Mark 1:21 report that Jesus taught in the synagogues of all the cities and villages in the region.

Luke opens and closes his Gospel in the temple (1:5–1 and 24:5–53); shows how God revealed his word and will in the temple when Jesus was dedicated (2:22–38); and stresses Jesus' involvement with synagogue and temple worship – 4:1–38, 44; 6:6; 13:10; 20:1

John builds his whole Gospel around the Jewish festivals, dividing Jesus' life into set periods. After describing the first week of Jesus' ministry, John comments on the events associated with a Passover (2:13–4:54), an unspecified festival but probably Purim (5:1–47), a second Passover (6:1–71), a feast of Tabernacles (7:1–10:21), a feast of Dedication (10:22–11:57), and a third Passover (13:1–19:4). We see in *Knowing the Son* that John's Gospel takes great pains to present Jesus as the fulfilment of all these important festivals.

Matthew 4:23 ☐
9:35 ☐

Mark 1:21 ☐

Luke 1:5–1 ☐
24:5–53 ☐
2:22–38 ☐
4:1–38 ☐
4:44 ☐
6:6 ☐
13:10 ☐
20:1 ☐

John 2:13 ☐
5:1 ☐
6:4 ☐
7:2 ☐
10:22 ☐
13:1 ☐

Acts 2:46 ☐

      3:1, 8 ☐

      5:12, 21 ☐

Acts 9:20 ☐

      13:14 ☐

Acts 2:46; 3:1, 8 and 5:12, 21 record that, even after Pentecost, the first believers continued to worship at the temple and synagogues.

The early chapters of Acts describe how the first converts were knitted together into a community which was characterised by:

- *worship in the temple*

- *generous giving* (we consider this in Part Seven)

- *eating together in each others' homes*

Acts 2:42–47 ☐

Acts 2:42–47 shows that their worship focused around *corporate prayer* and the *breaking of bread.* These activities helped to bind the believers into a united fellowship and to recognise their essential oneness in Christ – we consider this in *Glory in the Church.*

Acts 1:14–15 ☐

      2:42 ☐

      3:1 ☐

      4:24–25 ☐

      6:6 ☐

      12:12 ☐

      13:1–2 ☐

The emphasis on corporate prayer in worship can be seen throughout Acts, for example, 1:14–15; 2:42; 3:1; 4:24–25; 6:6; 12:12 and 13:1–2 – and we consider this in *Effective Prayer.* Acts does not tell us how the believers 'broke bread' or whether this was a celebration of 'the Lord's Supper', but there is no doubt that they did this almost every day, and that it was linked to their attendance at temple worship.

In time, however, the bitter antagonism of the Jews towards the disciples forced a break between the early church and official Judaism. This meant that the church had to develop new forms of worship which were not based in Jewish ritual, or on the Sabbath, or in the temple.

WORSHIP IN THE EARLY CHURCH

Acts 20:7 ☐

Although Acts 2:46 mentions daily services, Acts 20:7 suggests that the Lord's Day (Sunday, the first day of the week, the day of resurrection) had started to replace the Sabbath (Saturday, the last day of the week, the day of rest after creation) as a special day of worship.

The New Testament does not mention any special services to commemorate Jesus birth, resurrection or ascension, or to celebrate the outpouring of the Spirit at Pentecost; instead – as we stress in *Knowing the Son* – the early church focused entirely on remembering the Lord's death at the Lord's Supper.

It is clear that – after the break with Judaism – the early church worshipped in each other's homes and the open air. Their formal services were simple, and seem to have consisted mainly of praise, prayer, reading the Old Testament scriptures, and listening to instructions about the faith.

Psalms, hymns and songs

In Ephesians 5:19, the apostle Paul urges the believers to address one another in 'psalms and hymns and spiritual songs'. We can assume that Paul is referring to the Old Testament Psalms, but we cannot know what the difference is between the other two categories.

Ephesians 5:19 ☐

It may be that 'hymns' are known and recognised songs which are sung corporately; while 'spiritual songs' could be spontaneous, prophetic, Spirit-inspired songs which are sung individually – or they could also be praises which are sung corporately in tongues.

1 Corinthians 14:26 shows that singing was part of the church's regular worship, and this probably followed the common practice in Jewish synagogues. In *Knowing the Son*, we consider Philippians 2:6–11; Colossians 1:15–20 and 1 Timothy 3:16. Most scholars suggest that these are extracts from early Christian hymns which praise and honour Christ. It is also possible that Ephesians 5:14 is a verse from another early Christian hymn – one which urged believers into action.

1 Corinthians 14:26 ☐

Philippians 2:6–11 ☐

Colossians 1:15–20 ☐

1 Timothy 3:16 ☐

Ephesians 5:14 ☐

The ministry of the word

Even though Paul's letters were written essentially to non-Jewish, 'Gentile', believers, they contain very many allusions to the Jewish scriptures, to the Old Testament.

Because of this, it seems reasonable to assume that the regular reading of the Scriptures (just the Old Testament then) was an essential part of the early church's worship. Indeed, in 1 Timothy 4:13, Paul instructs Timothy to attend to the public reading of Scripture as well as to teaching and preaching.

1 Timothy 4:13 ☐

At some stage, church leaders also began to read publicly the letters and Gospels which now make up 'the New Testament'. In 1 Thessalonians 5:27, Paul asks for his letters to be read publicly in the

1 Thessalonians 5:27 ☐

Colossians 4:16 ☐

2 Thessalonians
            2:15 ☐

1 Timothy 5:18 ☐

Acts 20:7–11 ☐

Romans 10:9 ☐

Philippians 2:11 ☐

Romans 6:17 ☐

1 Corinthians
       15:1–8 ☐

Philippians 2:16 ☐

Ephesians 4:5 ☐

Philippians 1:27 ☐

Colossians 1:5 ☐
           2:6–7 ☐

2 Thessalonians
            2:12 ☐

Galatians 1:8 ☐

churches that he is addressing; and, in Colossians 4:16, he urges these churches to exchange his letters – and, presumably, to read them publicly as well.

2 Thessalonians 2:15 shows that Paul expected the believers to hold to the traditions that they had been taught by the apostles – whether orally or in writing. And 1 Timothy 5:18 shows that Paul could already refer to a saying of Jesus recorded by Luke as 'Scripture'.

It seems, therefore, that some accounts of Jesus' life and teaching were already being read in the church services, and that there must have been some element of teaching or instruction in the worship of the early church.

Although it is plain from passages like Acts 20:7–11 that extended times of teaching were, at times, part of the church's worship, Paul's letters appear to suggest that some of the teaching was given in the form of concise statements of doctrine which the believers memorised and declared together – we can call these 'confessional statements' or 'faith declarations'.

This has been the main way that traditional churches have taught the faith through the ages – especially to people who have few skills in reading and writing and little access to literature. It is the basis for most of the traditional liturgy which is still used in Anglican and Catholic churches, and it is an approach which many modern churches are beginning to rediscover.

In passages like Romans 10:9 and Philippians 2:11, Paul refers to brief confessions or declarations like 'Jesus is Lord'. And in Romans 6:17; 1 Corinthians 15:1–2 and Philippians 2:16 he seems to point to a central core of Christian teaching. Many scholars believe that 1 Corinthians 15:3–8 includes an example of a 'faith declaration' which the believers would have learnt and recited during worship.

In other places – for example, Ephesians 4:5; Philippians 1:27; Colossians 1:5; 2:6–7 and 2 Thessalonians 2:12 – Paul seems to use the phrases 'the faith' and 'the truth' to point to something more than the act of faith; and in Galatians 1:8 he refers to 'my gospel' in contrast to false gospels.

All this suggests that the early church's worship included simple statements of belief which helped to build faith, to develop oneness, and to instruct people in the truth about Jesus' death and resurrection.

Prayers

We study the apostle Paul's prayers – both for himself and for others – in some detail in *Effective Prayer*, and see the importance of the different forms of prayer (petition, intercession, warfare, and so on) in the life of Jesus and the early church. We also consider this in *Glory in the Church*.

In 1 Corinthians 1:2, Paul shows that 'calling on the name of the Lord' in prayer is one of the key hallmarks of true Christian believers, and he encourages people to keep on persisting in prayer in Colossians 4:2 and 1 Thessalonians 5:25.

The apostle Paul particularly stresses the importance of *thanksgiving*. We see this, for example, in 1 Corinthians 14:16; Philippians 4:6 and Colossians 4:2. This suggests that prayer in the church's worship was characterised by joyful gratitude at the amazing grace and goodness of God in Christ.

In passages like Romans 8:15; 1 Corinthians 16:22; 2 Corinthians 1:20 and Galatians 4:6, Paul seems to show that these non-Greek words were being widely used in the worship of the early church (Greek was the common language):

- *amen* – affirms the reliability of God's promises

- *maranatha* – affirms belief in the Lord's return

- *abba* – affirms the nature of God the Father

This suggests that these Aramaic words were being used in public worship then in much the same way as we still use them today.

Paul's epistles are letters of instruction, correction and direction to very young churches, and they deal only generally with the topics of personal and public worship. Paul never gives any detailed instructions about worship, and never imposes a precise order or form of worship. Instead, he simply pleads for simplicity and freedom in worship, and sets all his teaching about ethics and doctrine against a background of worship.

In particular, Paul teaches a great deal about 'baptism' and 'the Lord's Supper', and he always relates these 'sacraments' to public worship. We consider these in detail in *Glory in the Church*, but we should recognise here that Paul always sets them in the context of the public worship of the early church.

1 Corinthians 1:2 ☐

Colossians 4:2 ☐

1 Thessalonians 5:25 ☐

1 Corinthians 14:16 ☐

Philippians 4:6 ☐

Romans 8:15 ☐

1 Corinthians 16:22 ☐

2 Corinthians 1:20 ☐

Galatians 4:6 ☐

FREEDOM IN WORSHIP

1 Corinthians 11:2–14:40 ☐

The New Testament's most thorough teaching about worship is contained in Paul's first letter to the church at Corinth. In 1 Corinthians 11:2–14:40, Paul deals with a host of issues which had arisen in the fast-growing Greek city-church.

It seems that the church had been trying to put Paul's teaching into practice, but that three practical difficulties had arisen – difficulties which have repeatedly troubled congregations throughout the ages:

- *freedom and worship*
- *morals and worship*
- *spiritual gifts and worship*

Freedom

It seems the apostle Paul had taught the believers at the city of Corinth the same things that he had taught the churches in the rural area of Galatia. Two of Paul's most basic points were that:

Galatians 3:28 ☐
5:1 ☐

- *in Christ, there are no distinctions between class, race or gender* – Galatians 3:28
- *Christ has given believers a new freedom* – Galatians 5:1

In terms of public worship, this means that Paul allowed slaves, Gentiles and women to play a full part in every aspect of ministry – which was utterly contrary to the Jewish custom of his day.

1 Corinthians 11:2 shows that Paul had passed on 'traditions' to this effect to the Corinthian church. It seems that the church members had observed these traditions, but that they had misunderstood the true nature of Christian freedom.

Apparently, some women – who were taking a leading part in the church services – were doing in God's presence things that they would not have done in front of their pagan neighbours.

For example, the custom of the day laid down that respectable women did not appear in public with their heads uncovered. The Corinthian believers, however, argued that they had been set free from social rules and could express this freedom in the church.

Paul recognised that this was a similar problem to the one which had arisen in the church over food bought in pagan temples.

The only meat available for sale in Corinth came from the carcasses of animals which had been offered in sacrifice at the various temples. As the Jews would not supply the Christians with meat, and the Christians did not want to conform to the Jewish regulations, church members had to buy meat from pagan temples – or go without.

Some believers thought that it was wrong to eat this meat, and that they were endorsing and encouraging pagan worship. Paul deals with this in 1 Corinthians 8:1–11:1, where he makes four points.

1 Corinthians 8:1– 11:1 ☐

- *Believers are free to eat food offered to pagan gods because those gods do not exist. However, they must have a brotherly concern for believers who see the matter differently, and be ready sometimes to forgo food from pagan temples out of consideration for other believers.*

- *This was the kind of concession Paul had made in a different sphere. He had the right to be maintained financially by the believers, but he had voluntarily placed himself under restrictions so that his message might be accepted by all kinds of people.*

- *Christians should recognise that there could be real dangers in participating in pagan worship. They could not share in the Lord's Supper one day and in a pagan feast the next without grave spiritual consequences.*

- *The general principle is not to do anything which would lead other believers astray – even things which are right in themselves.*

In the case of the Corinthian women, Paul felt that they were offending *the society* that they were trying to reach with the gospel rather than other Christian believers.

He suggested, therefore, that – for the sake of the gospel, for the advancement of effective evangelism – any women taking a public part in the church's worship should follow the prevailing social custom and do so with their heads veiled.

This was always Paul's line: for example, he knew that believers had been set free from the need to be circumcised, but – in Acts 16:3 – he made sure that Timothy was circumcised so that they could reach the Jews more effectively with the gospel of freedom.

Acts 16:3 ☐

Morals

The apostle Paul was clearly concerned about the way that the Corinthian church was observing the Lord's Supper.

Instead of carrying out the instructions which Jesus had given, and which Paul had passed on to them at an earlier date, the Corinthian believers seem to have been turning the service into an occasion for feasting and fun. They were bringing along their own food to the Lord's Supper, and were having private feasts within the meeting instead of within their own homes.

The divisions within the church – which Paul had exposed and opposed – were also manifesting themselves during the public worship. As far as the apostle was concerned, the division and the ungodly revelry were dishonouring the Lord's Supper and the body of Christ.

Paul insisted that the Corinthians were not giving enough thought to their actions, and that they had brought the judgement of God down upon themselves.

1 Corinthians
10:16 ☐

In this important passage, Paul sets the Lord's Supper in the context of fellowship. As we see in *Glory in the Church*, *koinonia* – 'fellowship' or 'sharing' – is a key characteristic of the church, and in 10:16 Paul interprets the Supper in terms of *koinonia*, of sharing.

Paul shows that the Lord's Supper is in some way a sharing in the sacrifice of Christ. Just as the Jews relived the experiences of the exodus in the Passover, so believers participate in the sacrifice of Christ by identifying themselves with it in the Supper, and by committing themselves to the mission of Christ.

1 Corinthians
10:21 ☐
10:17 ☐

This is why Paul insists, in 10:21, that it is morally impossible to share in both the Lord's Supper and any form of idol worship. By fellowshipping in Christ's death through the Supper, we are automatically excluded from any fellowship which compromises our position in Christ.

Paul's one loaf and one body ideas in 10:17 make it clear that Christian fellowship includes *all* who participate in Christ, and that all are united in one loaf/body. According to Paul, therefore, the Lord's Supper has an in-built requirement for unity – which means that there are profound practical moral implications about sharing in the Supper. Quite simply, we should not dare to share in the Lord's Supper if we are not sharing with all others who fellowship in-and-with Christ.

In 11:29, Paul states that those who participate in the Supper without discerning the body are condemned – this presumably refers to those who do not maintain the purity of the body. Paul warns against having fellowship with immoral people throughout 1 Corinthians, and this illustrates just how seriously God views *koinonia*.

1 Corinthians
11:29 ☐

The fellowship aspect of the Lord's Supper was also affected by the Corinthians' wrong approach to the meal. Paul argues that the integrity of the body is violated when some eat well and others go hungry. The Lord's Supper should not focus on different styles of living, and Paul insists that those who are hungry should eat at home. This shows that the spiritual dimension of the Lord's Supper is paramount – arguments about the size of the bread and the flavour of the wine completely miss the spiritual point of the meal.

1 Corinthians contains Paul's clearest teaching about the Lord's Supper, and establishes that it should be central in Christian worship today. In 11:24–25 Paul stresses that the Supper is essentially an act of *memorial*.

1 Corinthians
11:24–26 ☐

In the Jewish Passover, the head of each household retold the story of the exodus to remind the worshippers that they were living in the good of those events. In the same way, during the Lord's Supper, worshippers are obliged to remember the cost of the Lord's death and to recognise that they are living in its achievements.

In 11:26, Paul shows that the memorial Supper is a proclamation and a participation, not a re-enactment. It proclaims the historic event at the centre of the Christian faith, within which we participate. The meal is not an attempt to keep alive something long dead, because it is not Christ's life which is remembered. The focus is on his saving death – an event of unique significance which reaches from the past, through the present, into the future, and forward into eternity.

Paul also shows that there is a future aspect to the Lord's Supper. In 11:26, he reveals that the memorial meal is to be the focus of church public worship only in the present age, for no memorial will be necessary when Christ returns and is present in person.

Spiritual gifts

The third practical difficulty that the Corinthians were facing in their public worship concerned spiritual gifts.

These were a fundamental part of the early church: they knew that they had been anointed with the Holy Spirit, and that the Holy Spirit inspired and empowered them to pray in tongues, to interpret tongues, to prophecy, to work miracles, to discern spirits, and so on. We consider these gifts in *Knowing the Holy Spirit*, *Listening to God* and *Ministry in the Spirit*.

It seems that the Corinthian believers were experiencing all these gifts of the Spirit, and were so eager to use them that several people were manifesting them publicly in church services at the same time.

The apostle Paul reminded them that God brings peace, not confusion. This means God ensures that – when spiritual gifts are manifested in public worship – they occur in a way which builds the whole body of the church.

Paul recognised the validity of all the gifts that were being manifested in the Corinthian services. He stressed that every one of them was God-given, and had a place in the public worship of the church.

He explained that just as the human body has different parts which all contribute to the effective functioning of the body, so the different gifts and members all contribute to the church's worship/service.

The key issue in all the Corinthians' practical problems was freedom in worship. Were the women free to flaunt the prevailing social convention during church services? Were different groups free to celebrate in the services with just their own group of friends? Were the people free to manifest spiritual gifts at the same time?

Paul's reply was to endorse their genuine freedom in Christ, but also to stress their over-riding responsibility to be motivated by the self-sacrificing love of God. As far as Paul is concerned:

- *women are free either to cover their heads or to leave them uncovered in the services; however, if they love the unbelievers in their midst with the love of God, they will not act in a way which erects any obstacles that might prevent the people from responding to the gospel*

- *people can eat what they like, when they like, with whom they like; if, however, they sincerely love each other with the love of God, they will not act in a way which erects or maintains barriers between different believers*

- *members can all manifest as many spiritual gifts as they are given; if, however, they really love the church with God's love, they will not act in a way which confuses other members but only in a way which edifies them and builds them together and up in Christ*

SACRIFICIAL WORSHIP

When we read through the Gospels and the book of Acts, it is plain that they ring with joy and praise.

When, for example, the Holy Spirit was poured onto the disciples at Pentecost, they were so overwhelmed with God's love that they worshipped him in new languages given to them by the Spirit.

Indeed, Romans 8:15–16 shows that whenever the Spirit enters the life of an individual, their natural response is to cry with joy, 'Abba, Father'; and Ephesians 5:18–20 shows that whenever the Spirit fills the life of a local church, its natural response in through exuberant praise and thanksgiving.

Romans 8:15–16 ☐

Ephesians
5:18–20 ☐

The truth, however, is that we do not always feel like this. If we worshipped God only when we felt like it, we might not worship him that often!

The New Testament acknowledges this truth by re-interpreting the Old Testament idea that true worship always involves sacrifice. It suggests that our worship in spirit and truth should be characterised by three main sacrifices, and we will consider these in more detail in the next three chapters.

The sacrifice of our bodies

The first eleven chapters of Paul's letter to the church in Rome is the fullest biblical description of the gospel. Romans 12:1 is Paul's 'therefore', his conclusion, to this description, in which he appeals to us to respond to the gospel with worship – by presenting our bodies as a 'living sacrifice'.

Romans 12:1 ☐

In those days, everyone was used to the idea of 'dead sacrifices' – which represented the total and unreserved surrender of something to God or a god. A 'living sacrifice', then, must involve the continuous surrender of a life to God in service.

Throughout Romans 12, Paul makes it clear that this involves being:

- *constantly transformed into the likeness of Christ*

- *totally committed to the body of Christ*

- *offering every God-given gift for the benefit of the whole church*

It involves love and service, prayer and patience, joy and hospitality, forgiveness and oneness, faith and hope, mercy and compassion, life and death, and so on.

Romans 15:16 ☐

Philippians 1:20 ☐
2:17 ☐

2 Timothy 4:6 ☐

Paul develops this idea in Romans 15:16, Philippians 1:20; 2:17 and 2 Timothy 4:6 by showing that the worship of God by the sacrifice of our bodies involves sacrificial service in the gospel of God which honours Christ – sometimes at great personal cost. We consider this aspect of worship in Part Six.

The sacrifice of our possessions

Hebrews 13:16 ☐

Hebrews 13:16 urges us to do good and share what we have as a sacrifice which is pleasing to God.

In *The Rule of God*, we consider Jesus' teaching about wealth, and see how he identifies it as a rival to God for our affections, and as a power which attempts to dominate and enslave us. Time and again, especially in the Gospel of Luke, Jesus looks for generosity in his followers.

2 Corinthians 8–9 ☐

The apostle Paul develops this in 2 Corinthians 8–9, where he urges the Corinthian believers to follow the example of the Macedonian churches. Although we consider this in detail later, we should recognise now that, in 2 Corinthians 9:11–13, Paul establishes a central place for sacrificial giving in Christian worship/service.

Throughout 2 Corinthians 8–9, Paul shows that the sacrifice of our possessions should be:

- *a response to God's love*

- *despite any hard times*

- *in proportion to our means*

- *with compassion for great need*

- *as an evidence of our commitment*

We consider the sacrifice of our possessions more fully in Part Seven.

The sacrifice of our praise

Hebrews 13:16 also encourages us to offer a sacrifice of praise to God with our lips. We have seen that Old Testament praise involved noise, music and movement, and that the early church was characterised by joy and thanksgiving.

The fact that praise is identified here as a sacrifice presupposes that some cost or effort is involved, and we consider this in Part Eight.

The New Testament reveals that the church is essentially a worshipping community of people who believe in Jesus. We are called together by him to worship him, and when we neglect our primary task we dishonour God and diminish ourselves.

As we move on to focus more on personal 'service' than on public 'worship' in the next three chapters, we should remember the three main principles of New Testament worship.

1. True worship is always directed towards the living God: it is not a performance to display human talents, it is an activity which glorifies only him, and which leads us deeper into his presence.

2. True worship always builds and edifies the whole body of Christ; it is not meant to be dominated by one or two specialists, it is the corporate expression of the praise of all God's people.

    In fact, 1 Corinthians 14:26 (almost the only verse in the New Testament to give explicit instructions about worship) suggests that – as far as possible – everyone should take an active part in church worship.

    1 Corinthians 14:26 ☐

3. True worship always depends on the presence of the Holy Spirit. As Paul says in Philippians 3:3, we must worship by the Spirit of God. Without him, we cannot communicate with God or offer him anything that is worthy of his name.

    Philippians 3:3 ☐

It is the Holy Spirit who inspires our prayer and praise, who opens our minds and helps us to understand God's word, who convicts us of sin and who gives gifts for the common good. Quite simply, he is the very breath of worship, and we consider him, and his role in worship, in Part Nine.

PART SIX

service and worship

We have seen that the Bible does not distinguish between 'spiritual worship' and 'practical service', and that it presents our worship of God as our service, and our service of God as our worship. Quite simply, the way that we serve him is the way that we worship him.

We have noted that the Hebrew word *abodah* and the Greek word *latreia* both originally signify the practical work of a slave or servant, but that they are also used in the Scriptures to describe service or worship of God: our service is our worship, and worship is our service.

And we have established that all God's commandments can be crystallised into worship and service. God's first priority for our lives is that we worship him with every part of our being; his second priority is that we serve others with the passion that we have for ourselves.

Service in spirit and truth

Service in spirit and truth always flows from worship in spirit and truth. Because worship and service are so closely intertwined that the Bible uses the same word for them, we can say that our worship is incomplete if it does not overflow into service; and that our service is unacceptable to God if it does not stem from our worship of God.

SERVICE WITH A TOWEL

The Gospels are painfully honest about the apostles' weaknesses and shortcomings. They describe their failures alongside their successes, their insights next to their arguments. It seems that they bickered more about their 'pecking order' than almost anything else, and Luke 9:46 candidly reports their argument about which of them was the greatest.

Luke 9:46 ☐

The greatest and the lowest

Whenever people are striving to be the greatest, they are also striving not to be the least. Although most of us know that we will never be the greatest, some believers still strive not to be the least. According to the Gospels, this was one of the apostles' main problems.

When the apostles gathered together with Jesus to celebrate the Passover, in John 13:1–17, they knew that one of them needed to wash the others' feet. (In those days, people reclined sideways on cushions, instead of sitting upright on chairs; so clean feet were very important at meal-times.) The problem was that foot-washing was a job for the lowest servant, and none of the apostles wanted to be that low.

John 13:1–17 ☐

John 13:2 suggests that they all preferred to sit through the meal with filthy feet than to be considered the least of the apostles. So Jesus took a towel, redefined greatness, elevated service, and revealed yet another crucial facet of the divine nature.

The context of worship

It is important we recognise that this all took place in the context of the most important act of worship in the Jewish year. Although the passover meal was eaten in homes, it was eaten during a worship service which contained hymns, readings, prayers and praise. Jesus' act of practical service flowed from this spiritual worship, and was part of the spiritual worship: truly, his service was his worship, and his worship was his service.

Having served the apostles, John 13:14–15 records that Jesus then called them to the way of similar service. It seems, however, that some believers would rather be called to radical self-denial for the sake of the gospel than to seemingly insignificant service like washing feet.

But Jesus does not call his followers only to glorious praise, dangerous mission and difficult tasks, he also calls us to the mundane and the ordinary, to the trivial and the easy, to the insignificant and the overlooked.

Leadership and authority

In several books in this *Sword of the Spirit* series, especially in *Knowing the Son*, we see how the four Gospels complement each other by focusing on different aspects of Jesus' nature and mission. We have seen, for example, that Matthew stresses Jesus' authority, Mark his service, Luke his humanity and John his divinity.

It is all the more remarkable then, that it is John's Gospel – and not Mark or Luke – which records this incident. Throughout his Gospel, John takes great pains to present Jesus as fully divine, as the complete revelation of God, as one in nature and person with the Father, as the 'I am' who revealed himself to Moses in the wilderness, and so on.

This means that Jesus' act of service with the towel is not just an example of ideal human behaviour; more importantly, it is also a dynamic revelation of God's way of behaving: it shows us how 'the Lord and Teacher', the 'I am he', exercises his sovereign leadership and his absolute authority.

When Jesus picked up the towel and washed his disciples feet, he was not abolishing leadership and authority, he was redefining them. He was showing that service is for masters as much as it is for servants. Jesus always taught and revealed an authority which was based in function rather than in status, and a leadership which served people instead of manipulating and controlling them. We see this, for example, in Matthew 20:25–28.

Matthew
20:25–28 ☐

This suggests that true spiritual authority is found more in a towel and a bar of soap than in a position and a title.

SELF-RIGHTEOUS SERVICE

If we are to understand and practise 'service in spirit and truth' we must distinguish it from 'self-righteous service'.

Human effort

Self-righteous service always comes through human effort: it calculates and schemes about how and who to serve. In contrast, true service flows from worship, from the promptings of God which are heard when we bow in his presence. We consider this more fully in *The Rule of God* and in *Listening to God*.

We serve in spirit and truth only because we have listened to God and have been directed and equipped by him.

Seeks to be noticed

Self-righteous service is ostentatious service which hopes to be noticed and is impressed by great acts of service. True service, however, does not distinguish small acts of service from large acts of service; it indiscriminately welcomes all opportunities to serve – no matter how small and hidden.

Self-righteous service always wants to be seen and noticed, to be applauded and rewarded. But true service does not seek attention: it is content with human hiddenness and values divine approval more than human praise.

Selective and temporary

Self-righteous service is concerned with results and is selective about whom is served, while true service delights in serving and serves enemies as willingly as friends, the low as well as the high, the ungrateful as well as the generous.

Self-righteous service is just a temporary action which is affected by feelings and desires, but true service is a permanent life-style which is governed only by God.

Self-gratification

Ultimately, self-righteous service is a form of self-gratification and self-glorification. It manipulates and controls people, and damages the community.

True service, however, cares for the needs of others with the passion that we have for ourselves. It obliges nobody to return the service, builds the body of Christ and brings great glory to God.

EXPRESSIONS OF SERVICE

Just as we can be tempted to understand worship in terms of 'what we do in church on Sunday', so it can be easy to think of service simply as a list of things that we could or should do.

But just as our worship is more than our singing, praying and listening, so our service is more than our cleaning, caring and cooking.

We have seen that 'worship in spirit and truth' is a continuous way of living before God, that it is a permanent inner attitude of loving adoration and holy awe. So too 'service in spirit and truth' is a way of living rather than a code of ethics or a check list of deeds. We should never forget that it is one thing to act like a servant when we feel like it, but quite another thing to be a servant all the time.

It is not enough, though, to stress only the inner nature of service. For just as our worshipping attitude needs to be expressed in music, movement, noise, prayer, praise and thanksgiving, so too our serving attitude needs to be expressed in the church and the world around us.

The Scriptures do not contain the serving equivalent of the book of Psalms, instead it leavens itself continuously with examples of serving which almost pass unnoticed.

Simple tasks

When, for example, we think about those whom God used to bring us the New Testament, we usually think of the apostle Paul. His writings have literally changed the world and transformed millions and millions of lives. How many of us pause to thank God for the quiet service of Tychicus?

It seems that Paul wrote most of his letters when he was in prison, and could not deliver them in person. As there was no postal service in those days, Paul often asked his friend Tychicus to travel hundreds of miles by foot to deliver them. We see this, for example, in Ephesians 6:21; Colossians 4:7; 2 Timothy 4:12 and Titus 3:12.

Most scholars think that Ephesians was written as a 'circular' letter which was sent to many churches, and it is possible that Tychicus traipsed all over Asia Minor delivering a pile of copies of 'Ephesians' to all the different churches in the area.

His was an anonymous, hidden, lonely, simple deed of service which would have seemed both mundane and insignificant at the time – literally anyone could have done it. And yet we would not have the New Testament today if Tychicus had not served with such faithfulness.

Active helpfulness

Of course, most acts of service do not have such enormous consequences.

Acts 9:39, for example, records how Dorcas served in a very small way which impacted just a few needy people in her immediate locality. But the Holy Spirit has seen fit to highlight her service in the Scriptures as an example for us all to follow.

We must learn from the Holy Spirit himself. He is the humble, self-effacing Spirit who exists to focus attention on the Son rather than on himself. When we live in the realm of the Spirit, we soon discover that the real issues are found in the tiny corners of other people's lives where small things are central and self is secondary.

At the most basic level, service in spirit and truth is just active helpfulness, providing simple assistance in trifling, external matters – opening a door, making coffee, wiping the dishes, and so on.

We must never forget that Christ has shown us in the sign of the towel that *nobody* is too important or too busy for the lowliest acts of service.

Ephesians 6:21 ☐
Colossians 4:7 ☐
2 Timothy 4:12 ☐
Titus 3:12 ☐

Acts 9:39 ☐

Accepting service

At a different level, service involves being served and accepting service. Peter did not want Jesus to wash his feet because he was humble but because he was proud, for Jesus' service was an affront to Peter's idea of authority and leadership. If Peter had been in charge, there is no chance that he would have washed anyone's feet!

When we allow others to serve us we are recognising their authority over us, and we receive it without feeling a need to repay it in turn.

Providing hospitality

Hospitality is almost the only expression of service which is expressly urged upon us in the Scriptures. 1 Peter 4:9 encourages this in all believers, and Romans 12:13; 1 Timothy 3:2 and Titus 1:8 make it a pre-condition of church leadership.

1 Peter 4:9 ☐

Romans 12:13 ☐

1 Timothy 3:2 ☐

Titus 1:8 ☐

The Scriptures are packed with examples of hospitality, from Rachel's protection of the spies, through Boaz's provision for Ruth and Naomi, and the widows' care for Elijah and Elisha, to Mary and Martha's welcome to Jesus and his disciples.

When Jesus sent the twelve and the seventy to preach the gospel, he commanded them to depend on hospitality, and we see that this instruction was obeyed throughout the book of Acts. It may be that the modern business culture of staying in hotels and eating at restaurants has robbed us of much of the biblical joy which was found in giving and receiving hospitality.

WORSHIP, SERVICE AND HUMILITY

It should be plain by now that worship/service is an essentially humble activity. We have seen that *shachah* and *proskuneo* – bowing down – are basic biblical words for worship/service, and that God's worshippers/servants must have an attitude of bowing before him if they are to offer him the worship/service that he expects and deserves.

Developing humility

It can seem hard to develop humility. In fact we can seem almost 'unhumble' if we consciously seek humility. Nevertheless, when we set out on a course of action which stresses hiddenness and which focuses on the good of others, we can expect the Holy Spirit to work his humility into our lives.

Fallen, fleshly humanity rejects service and hiddenness, and longs instead for comfort and recognition. But these are desires which we must 'crucify' as hard and as persistently as wrong sexual desires. Passages like 1 John 2:16 do not refer only to sexuality, but to every human emotion and activity which is not under God's full control.

1 John 2:16 ☐

Many people struggle with wrong desires, and do not know how to deal with them. Throughout church history, many different groups of believers have discovered that a balanced mixture of spiritual worship and hidden service is the best way to control fleshly desires and develop a godly attitude of healthy humility.

This was the mainspring of all the early monastic movements that God used to spread the gospel throughout Europe and to plant the first churches in Britain and Ireland.

During the 18th Century, when God again sent revival to Britain through men like Wesley and Whitfield, he inspired a man from a very different church tradition to write one of the most influential Christian books of all time – 'A serious call to a devout and holy life'.

William Law taught that believers should view every day as 'a day of humility' and as 'a day for serving others'. Remarkably, while God used Wesley to sweep hundreds of thousands of new converts into the church, he simultaneously used Law to usher in a fresh wave of holiness within the church.

Law insisted that we can develop the humility that God is seeking in true worshippers when we:

'condescend to all the weaknesses and infirmities of your fellow creatures, cover their frailties, love their excellencies, encourage their virtues, relieve their wants, rejoice in their prosperities, compassionate their distresses, receive their friendship, overlook their unkindness, forgive their malice, be a servant of servants, and condescend to do the lowest offices to the lowest of mankind.'

When we start to obey God and serve others with the passion that we have for ourselves, we will find that the humility of *shachah* and *proskuneo* will start to blossom in our lives.

We will begin to be less hurried and more at peace. We will start to view with compassion those whom we once envied. We will begin to be interested in those whom we used to ignore. And we will be filled with a new sense of identification with the *ptochos* – 'the hurting' whom Jesus came to reach and to save.

But more important than all this, the humility of *shachah* and *proskuneo* will turn us into true worshippers who are far more aware of God, and who are much quicker and keener to praise him. Hidden service will be an enacted prayer of thanksgiving, as our spiritual worship overflows into practical service, and as our service leads us directly to God in praise and adoration.

PART SEVEN

giving and worship

We have seen that the New Testament urges us to offer God three sacrifices in worship:

- *the sacrifice of our bodies*

- *the sacrifice of our possessions*

- *the sacrifice of our praise*

Although we are considering these aspects of worship separately – in this, the last and the next chapters – we must appreciate that they are three complementary, overlapping aspects of worship/service in spirit and in truth.

God is not calling us to choose between hidden acts of service and generous giving, or between joyful praise and practical helpfulness; he is calling us to worship/serve him with every part of our beings – and this involves serving *and* giving *and* praising. If we neglect any one aspect, we will not be worshipping him in spirit and truth.

We have also seen that worship is our human response to God's revelatory initiative, and that our response is determined by the nature of God. For example, we respond with holy worship because God has shown that he is holy; we respond with self-sacrifice because God has revealed himself as the self-sacrificing God; we respond with praise because God has shown that he is filled with joy and praise; we respond with foot-washing service because he has revealed himself to be the God who washes dirty feet; and we respond to him with giving because everything God does reveals that he is the giving God.

Whether we think about God in terms of creation or redemption, grace or love, truth or mercy, we can always see that he is a holy giver.

OLD TESTAMENT GIVING

In the Old Testament, God's people responded to God's gracious generosity with three forms of giving:

- *sacrifices to God*

- *tithes to the poor and to the religious leaders*

- *freewill offerings for special projects*

Sacrifices

Sacrifices were gifts which were given directly to God: we have considered them in Part Three and we study them in more detail in *Salvation by Grace*. We have seen that whenever the people of Israel turned to God, they worshipped him by offering him sacrifices.

Some believers seem to think that the Jews offered God sacrifices only to deal with their sin. But the Old Testament shows that they gave sacrificially to God when they rejoiced as well as when they wept – they gave him their best in thanksgiving, dedication, intercession, praise and worship – as well as in repentance and with pleas for forgiveness.

Tithes

The tithe was an annual gift of 10% of the family income which was given to provide an income for the poor and for the religious leaders.

The Old Testament does not set out the precise arrangements for the collection of tithes, and the practice seems to have changed through the centuries. Leviticus 27:30–32, however, makes it plain that all crops and all animals had to be tithed.

Leviticus 27:30–32 ☐

Whenever the people harvested their crops, one tenth had to be given away. And, once a year, families counted their animals as they walked to pasture. Every tenth animal was given away to ensure that a fair selection was made: they could not use the tithe to dispose of their inferior animals, but they did not have to select the best – as with a sacrifice.

It is important we appreciate that the value of what families offered in sacrifice during the year was not deducted from the tithe. They gave their sacrifices from the nine-tenths of their income which was left-over *after* they had given their tithe.

Leviticus 27:30 and Malachi 3:6–12 show that the tithe belonged to God and was given to God. Unlike sacrifices, however, tithes were God's special provision for particular groups of people.

Malachi 3:6–12 ☐

For two years in three, families gave their tithes to the levites and priests who were responsible for the worship of the nation; and, in the third year, they gave it to the poor in their own locality. Numbers 18:21–32 and Deuteronomy 14:29 explain why the tithes were given to theses groups of people.

Numbers 18:21–32 ☐

Deuteronomy 14:29 ☐

It is important to note that Old Testament tithes were not used to pay for buildings or special projects – these were financed by freewill offerings. Instead, tithes were used entirely to provide an income for people involved in ministry and for those who were in desperate need.

Freewill offerings

Freewill offerings were usually given for special projects – especially to erect and maintain special buildings. For example:

- *the tabernacle offering* – Exodus 25:1–4; 35:1–29; 36:2–7

Exodus 25:1–4 ☐
35:1–29 ☐
36:2–7 ☐

- *the first temple offering* – 1 Chronicles 28–29

1 Chronicles 28–29 ☐

- *the second temple offering* – Ezra 1:2–6; 2:68–69; 3:5; 7:16; Nehemiah 7:70–72

Ezra 1:2–6 ☐
2:68–69 ☐
3:5 ☐
7:16 ☐

Nehemiah 7:70–72 ☐

These offerings were not tithes, for the people did not have to give a fixed percentage of their income. They were 'freewill', so the people did not have to contribute: those with willing hearts were asked to give as much or as little as they chose. The offerings were always very specific – the people knew what was needed and how their gifts would be used – and they ended when enough had been given.

God's people were also under a duty to provide generously for the poor through regular freewill offerings – we see this, for example, in Deuteronomy 10:17–19; 15:7–11; 24:10–22 and Isaiah 58:6–11.

Deuteronomy
10:17–19 ☐
15:7–11 ☐
24:10–22 ☐

Isaiah 58:6–11 ☐

GIVING AND JESUS

We have often noted in this *Sword of the Spirit* series that Jesus taught more about financial matters than any subject other than the kingdom of God. Jesus gave a great deal of time to dealing with the issue of money, and Mark 12:41 reports that he watched what people gave when they came to worship, that he discerned the spirit in which they gave, and that he commented on the level of their giving.

Mark 12:41 ☐

Matthew 6:24 is the basis of all Jesus' teaching about money: he insists that it is a power – a false god – which seeks to dominate and enslave people. This explains why we find it so hard to give money away, and why so much of Jesus' teaching about money is given in an evangelistic setting.

Matthew 6:24 ☐

Jesus' teaching about giving

In Luke 3:8–11, John the Baptist teaches that giving should be the first-fruit of our repentance, and Jesus repeatedly stresses that giving is part of our commitment to him. We see this, for example, in Matthew 19:23–26; Luke 5:1–11; 12:33–34 and 18:18–23.

Luke 3:8–11 ☐

Matthew
19:23–26 ☐

Luke 5:1–11 ☐
12:33–34 ☐
18:18–23 ☐

In his famous parable of the sheep and the goats in Matthew 25:31–46, Jesus makes it plain that God wants us to give generously to the needy. And in Luke 11:42, he stresses that – on its own – careful tithing is not enough, we must give freewill gifts to the needy as well: this principle is dramatically illustrated in Luke 10:29–37.

Matthew
25:31–46 ☐

Luke 11:42 ☐

Luke 10:29–37 ☐

Luke 16 contains Jesus most thorough teaching about the use of money – which he illustrates with the story about a rich man and Lazarus. His starkest teaching on giving is contained in the Sermon on the Mount, in Matthew 5:42. Jesus repeats this basic principle in Luke 6:30–38 (we must never forget that the rewards promised in verse 38 relate to the giving demanded in verse 30).

In Matthew 6:1–3, Jesus follows his teaching on giving by describing how we should give. He explains that we forfeit our heavenly reward when we attract attention to our giving.

Luke 14:12–14 records Jesus' instructions about hospitality: once again, he shows that God wants us to make giving to the needy our priority – for in this way we are giving to God. Matthew 17:24–27; 22:15–22, Mark 12:13–17 and Luke 20:20–26 show that Jesus also taught the people to pay their taxes – and that he paid them himself.

Jesus' giving encounters

The Gospels record many occasions when people give to Jesus, when he urges people to give, and when he comments upon people's giving. For example:

- *wise men worshipped Jesus by giving gifts* – Matthew 2:9–12

- *women worshipped Jesus by anointing him with ointment* – Matthew 26:6–13, Mark 14:3–9, Luke 7:36–50; John 12:1–11

- *women gave practically to support Jesus' ministry* – Luke 8:1–3; 10:38–42; John 11:1–45; 12:1–12

- *Joseph gave Jesus his tomb* – Matthew 27:57–60; Mark 15:42–47; Luke 23:50–54

- *Cleopas and his companion gave Jesus a meal* – Luke 24:13–35

- *a rich man refused to give as Jesus directed* – Matthew 19:16–22; Mark 10:17–22; Luke 18:18–23

- *Zacchaeus gave more than Jesus directed* – Luke 19:1–10

- *a boy gave his lunch to Jesus* – John 6:9

- *a widow gave her all in worship* – Mark 12:41–44; Luke 21:1–4

- *a leper obeyed Jesus and gave in thanksgiving* – Matthew 8:1–4; Mark 1:40–44 and Luke 5:12–14

Luke 16 ☐
Matthew 5:42 ☐
Luke 6:30–38 ☐
Matthew 6:1–3 ☐
Luke 14:12–14 ☐
Matthew
        17:24–27 ☐
        22:15–22 ☐
Mark 12:13–17 ☐
Luke 20:20–26 ☐
Matthew 2:9–12 ☐
Matthew 26:6–13 ☐
Mark 14:3–9 ☐
Luke 7:36–50 ☐
John 12:1–11 ☐
Luke 8:1–3 ☐
        10:38–42 ☐
John 11:1–45 ☐
        12:1–12 ☐
Matthew
        27:57–60 ☐
Mark 15:42–47 ☐
Luke 23:50–54 ☐
Luke 24:13–35 ☐
Matthew
        19:16–22 ☐
Mark 10:17–22 ☐
Luke 18:18–23 ☐
Luke 19:1–10 ☐
John 6:9 ☐
Mark 12:41–44 ☐
Luke 21:1–4 ☐
Matthew 8:1–4 ☐
Mark 1:40–44 ☐
Luke 5:12–14 ☐

The gifts of the boy and the widow are particularly important. From an earthly perspective, both looked tiny; from a heavenly perspective, however, they were huge. According to Jesus, the woman's two coins – the smallest of her day – were worth more than all the contributions of all the other worshippers added together!

This shows that God does not measure what we give in worship; he measures what we keep back. The boy's gift may have looked small on earth; but – because he gave all he had – it was enormous in heaven. In the miracle of the feeding of the 5,000, Jesus made the boy's lunch appear as large on earth as it was in reality in heaven. He enabled the people to benefit from the spiritual size of the boy's gift.

This means that those who give the least may actually be giving the most, and that those who donate large gifts may really be giving only a tiny amount. We do not need to worry about giving a small sum of money – if that is all we have – for God can use it in an enormous way.

GIVING AND THE EARLY CHURCH

Acts 2:1–4 □

The story of the early church begins with a special gift from God. Acts 2:1–4 describes how God gave himself, his Spirit, his power, and so on. He gave this freely, without any pre-conditions, to the same people who had deserted and denied his Son only a few weeks before.

As a direct consequence of God's giving, about three thousand people believed and were baptised that day. This is the first appearance of the New Testament principle that gifts and giving lead to growth.

The giving community

Acts 2:42–47 □

Acts 2:42–47 describes what happened to the new converts. Their repentance was evidenced by a change in financial behaviour, and giving was central to their lives which were now committed to Christ.

When they saw a need, they gave to meet that need, and this giving led to praise and worship. Their generosity made them glad, it greatly impressed other people, and it led to considerable church growth.

Acts 3:1–9 shows that the giving community was led by generous leaders, for it records how Peter and John gave to a lame beggar. They did not ignore the needy man, and they did not give him their small change; instead, they promised to give him whatever they had. We must not be so excited by the healing miracle that we overlook their giving spirit.

Acts 4:32–35 describes the believers' generosity. Again, we must take care not to lift the apostles' testimony out of the context of this giving. The believers' giving was part of the testimony to Jesus' resurrection. They were giving sacrificially in response to Jesus' sacrificial gift; their generosity proved that Jesus was alive.

There is an important development in these verses. For the first time, the early church started to organise giving so that gifts were used more efficiently. Instead of giving only directly to the poor, believers *also* gave to a central fund which directed their giving to the most needy.

In the Old Testament, the people's 'third year' tithes were collected together in each town to create a common store from which the poor could be fed – and the early church seems to have followed this pattern.

Ananias and Sapphira

Luke – the writer of Acts – appears to present several deliberate contrasts in both his books. We have seen that he contrasted the rich young ruler with Zacchaeus, and in Acts 4:36–5:11 he seems to contrast Barnabas with Ananias and Sapphira.

Barnabas sold a field and gave all the proceeds to the church's common fund. Ananias and Sapphira also sold some possessions, but they gave only a part to the fund. They wanted the public esteem of giving generously, but they could not bear to part with all their money.

Peter makes it plain, in Acts 5:4, that Ananias and Sapphira were under no obligation to sell their possession, and that it would have been in order for them to give only part of the proceeds. But they had lied – because they could not admit that they would not give all.

The deaths of Ananias and Sapphira in 5:5–11 are a terrible warning about giving. Just as Israel's story begins with God's rejection of Cain's gift, so the story of the church also begins with God's rejection of a couple whose giving was unacceptable to him.

Acts 3:1–9 ☐

Acts 4:32–35 ☐

Acts 4:36–5:11 ☐

Acts 6:1–7 ☐

Luke 7:5–6 ☐
8:1–3 ☐
19:8–10 ☐
21:1–4 ☐
23:50–54 ☐

Acts 4:36–37 ☐
9:36–39 ☐
10:1–2 ☐
11:27–30 ☐

Giving problems

Acts 6:1–7 describes one of the early church's first problems. The numbers of converts had grown so fast that, despite the common fund, a group of widows were being overlooked in the daily food distribution. There was so much for the apostles to do that they could not manage to preach and distribute the funds efficiently.

The apostles solved their problem by delegating. They chose seven Spirit-filled men to be jointly responsible for the finances and for ensuring that the people's giving was properly administered.

As a result of taking their giving so seriously, the word of God increased and the numbers of disciples multiplied greatly in Jerusalem.

Giving believers

It seems that, as far as Luke is concerned, generosity is the basic characteristic of the Christian believer. In his Gospel, he repeatedly comments about a person's giving – for example, the Capernaum centurion in 7:5–6, Joanna and Susanna in 8:1–3, Zacchaeus in 19:8–10, the widow in 21:1–4, and Joseph in 23:50–54.

It is much the same in his second book – for example, Barnabas in Acts 4:36–37, Dorcas in Acts 9:36–39 and Cornelius in Acts 10:1–2.

Giving to people far away

Acts 11:27–30 records an important development in giving. Barnabas and Paul were teaching Gentile believers in Syrian Antioch – almost 400 miles north of Jerusalem – when they were visited by some prophets who foretold a great famine.

The prophets did not tell the Antioch believers what to do, they simply made them aware of a forthcoming need. The disciples decided for themselves to meet this need with a freewill offering for the believers in Israel.

Until this point, giving had always been for local needs. Tithes, sacrifices and offerings had been given for local leaders and for the poor in the immediate locality. The believers now realised, however, that they also had a responsibility for needy people whom they could not see and had never met.

Interestingly, these Antioch givers were the first people to be called Christians. If we choose to call ourselves by their name, perhaps we should choose to give like them too.

Paul's giving good-bye

Acts 20:17–37 records Paul's farewell sermon to the Ephesian believers whom he had served for over two years. He could have preached about anything, but he chose to teach about giving. He could have picked any text, but he chose some words of Jesus about giving.

Giving was so high on Paul's priorities that he made it the last thing he said to the disciples. Whenever these Ephesians remembered Paul in the future, they would be sure to recall his farewell sermon.

This particular saying of Jesus does not appear in the Gospels. But it encapsulates the teaching of Jesus and Paul – and the life of the early church. They knew that giving brought happiness, and they recognised that giving brought growth – and was God's way for his people.

Paul's choice of sermon should not surprise us, for the book of Acts records that he was always keen to raise money for others. We have seen that he was at Antioch when they gave generously for famine relief, and he took the money with Barnabas to Jerusalem. Passages like Romans 12:8, 13, 20 and 15:27–29 reflect Paul's concern for believers to give generously.

Tithes and sacrifices

We have seen that the first believers still paid their tithes to the Jewish religious leaders and made their sacrifices in the Jerusalem temple. They did this because they were Jews.

However, when the Gentiles were welcomed as believers, there was some dispute as to which Jewish regulations they should observe. After a conference at Jerusalem, the apostles decided that Gentile believers need abstain only from illicit marriages, anything polluted by idols, and the meat of strangled animals. They did not have to offer sacrifices, or be circumcised, or to tithe according to the law of Moses.

But even though the early church did not have a legalistic system of tithing, they still recognised that the people who ministered should be

Acts 20:17–37 ☐

Romans 12:8 ☐
12:13 ☐
12:20 ☐
15:27–29 ☐

1 Timothy 5:17 ☐

Romans 12:1 ☐

Ephesians 5:1–2 ☐

Philippians
4:15–20 ☐

Hebrews 13:16 ☐

1 Timothy 6:2–13 ☐

2 Peter 2:3 ☐

1 Timothy
6:17–19 ☐

Revelation
3:15–22 ☐

2 Corinthians 8–9 ☐

provided with a proper income. Paul makes this clear in 1 Timothy 5:17.

And when they stopped offering God sacrifices in the temple, they started giving him other forms of sacrifice. We see this, for example, in Romans 12:1; Ephesians 5:1–2; Philippians 4:15–20 and Hebrews 13:16.

False teachers

There was obviously a danger that some leaders would abuse Paul's teaching about 'double honour' and press believers to give to them personally. The New Testament points to this danger and names such men as false teachers – in, for example, 1 Timothy 6:2–13 and 2 Peter 2:3.

Rich Christians

There are some believers who – like Barnabas, Zacchaeus, Mary and Martha – are affluent. God has blessed them financially.

1 Timothy 6:17–19 contains the apostle Paul's directions for them. He does not order them to give all their money away and become poor; instead, he reminds them about their special responsibility to be generous, and the danger of depending on the wrong sort of riches.

Revelation 3:15–22 reports that the church at Laodicea was prosperous, but it was condemned for trusting in the wrong sort of riches – not for being wealthy.

Generous giving

We have already seen that 2 Corinthians 8–9 contains more teaching about giving than any other part of the New Testament.

In these important chapters, the apostle Paul urges the Corinthian believers to match the Philippian believers' giving, and gives three reasons why the Corinthians should give with great generosity:

- *to prove that their love is genuine*

- *to follow the example of Christ*

- *to bring equality between the saints*

Paul ends these two chapters on giving, in 9:6–15, with a series of important pleas and promises. Most importantly, he concludes by showing emphatically that our giving should be a response of thanksgiving to God's giving and that it precipitates praise, thanksgiving and worship among others.

PART EIGHT

rejoicing and worship

Proverbs 8 and 9 are some of the most remarkable prophetic chapters in the Bible. As we see in *Ministry in the Spirit*, most Old Testament prophets speak the word of *Yahweh* and announce his thoughts. In contrast, Proverbs 8:4–36; 9:4–12 report the words of *Wisdom*.

In implying that *Wisdom* is a being who is both 'divine' and 'distinct from God', Proverbs 8:22–30 is one of a small number of Old Testament passages which suggest that God is 'more than One' in nature. We consider this more fully in *Knowing the Father*.

We see in *Knowing the Son* that most Old Testament prophecies point to the Messiah, to God's servant, to David's son, to Jesus. Proverbs 8 and 9 go even further than this, for they reproduce the words of Jesus himself before his incarnation. Close study of these chapters shows that the words of *the Wisdom of God* are remarkably echoed and fulfilled in the teaching of *the Word of God* in John's Gospel.

Proverbs 8:22–31 is the plainest biblical description of God's activity before the creation. Verse 30 shows that rejoicing in a relationship was at the heart of God's life then; it, therefore – because of his self-consistency – must be at the heart of his life today and forever.

God did not create the world because he was bored, he made it because he was rejoicing in the relationships within himself. The variety, the life, the beauty of creation is simply an expression or overflow of God's joy in-and with himself.

Verse 31 describes God rejoicing in the new world – and this pleasure is evident in Genesis 1's oft-repeated observation that God found it all 'good'.

THE JOY OF THE LORD

Luke 2:10 ☐

19:37 ☐

John 15:11 ☐

This divine joy is at the heart of Jesus' life. Luke 2:10 reports that he entered the world on a note of great jubilation; Luke 19:37 describes the people's joy when he entered Jerusalem; and John 15:11 shows him bequeathing his joy to the disciples as he prepares to leave the world.

In particular, the first two chapters of Luke's Gospel are set against a backdrop of intense rejoicing. For example:

Luke 1:14 ☐

1:28 ☐

1:44 ☐

1:47 ☐

1:58 ☐

1:64 ☐

2:10 ☐

2:13 ☐

2:20 ☐

2:38 ☐

- *the angel tells Zechariah that many will rejoice at the birth of his son* – 1:14

- *the angel's first words to Mary are 'Rejoice!'* – 1:28

- *Elisabeth and her unborn child rejoice when they see Mary and realise whom she is carrying* – 1:44

- *Mary rejoices* – 1:47

- *the neighbours rejoice* – 1:58

- *Zechariah rejoices* – 1:64

- *the angel brings the shepherds news of great joy – a joy which is to be shared with the whole people* – 2:10

- *the host of heaven rejoice* – 2:13

- *the shepherds rejoice* – 2:20

- *Anna rejoices* – 2:38

The year of Jubilee

Luke uses this general air of rejoicing to prepare the way for Jesus' announcement in Luke 4:18–19 – which we consider in *Reaching the Lost*.

Luke 4:18–19 ☐

Many scholars are convinced that Jesus' 'mission statement' was a proclamation of a new year of Jubilee. In Luke 4:19, Jesus states that he has been anointed with the Spirit to announce 'the acceptable year of the Lord'. This is 'the year of the Lord's favour', the year which God has graciously appointed to show his salvation.

This does seem to point to 'the year of jubilee' which was established in Leviticus 25. This was a year of liberation, which was held every fifty years, when fields were left fallow, debts were forgiven, slaves set free, and all property was returned to its original owner.

Leviticus 25 ☐

If this is right, it means that 'the year of jubilee' – like all the other ritual feasts, sacrifices and ceremonies of the Old Testament – was a prophetic symbol or foreshadowing of the reality of Jesus' saving mission. As wonderful as the year of jubilee was, it was only a pointer to the ultimate jubilee which was announced and fulfilled by Jesus.

The year of jubilee was a time of endless jubilation which celebrated the generous, gracious provision of God. Leviticus 25:21 shows that he could be trusted to provide what was needed, and the year-long rejoicing was founded on this freedom from worry and care.

If Jesus was declaring that he had been anointed to usher in the ultimate year of jubilee, it means that the age of salvation was meant to be enjoyed with unceasing rejoicing which is based on God's gracious provision.

It should be obvious that jubilation, great rejoicing, is the only appropriate response when the poor and the hurting hear the Good News, when the captives are released, when the blind receive their sight, and when the oppressed are liberated.

Of course, there are enormous social implications in the concept of a perpetual year of jubilee, for we cannot simply 'spiritualise' the regular restructuring of social arrangements to bring about greater equality.

Jesus' salvation has brought about a degree of forgiveness, healing, deliverance and equality which was unimaginable in the Old Testament jubilees. His salvation, however, has not abolished the social dimensions of the Old Testament jubilees; instead, it has fulfilled and completed them, and has raised them to a much higher level.

No matter how hard it is for us to understand and work through the 'world' dimensions of salvation that we consider in *Knowing the Father*, we must never forget that Jesus was inaugurating perpetual jubilation. According to Jesus, the age of salvation, the age of the Spirit, the age of the church, is meant to be an age of great rejoicing.

The jubilation which is at the centre of God's being is meant to fill his people. The joy that God enjoyed within himself is meant to be our joy in him. The joy that he expressed at the sight of his original creation is meant to be our joy in each other and all creation. The joy that he articulated at the sight of his Son at his baptism and transfiguration is meant to be our joy in his Son and his glory, and so on.

We have seen that our response to God should be determined by his revelation to us – that we give because he gives, serve because he serves, sacrifice because he has sacrificed, and so on. In the same way, our response to his revelation of his joy and jubilation should be to live in the perpetual jubilee of the Spirit with great rejoicing.

BIBLICAL JOY

Psalm 16:11 ☐

Romans 15:13 ☐

Philippians 4:4 ☐

1 Peter 1:8 ☐

Revelation 19:7 ☐

In the Scriptures, joy is always a quality rather than merely an emotion. It is based in God, is derived from him, is a defining characteristic of his people, and is a foretaste of the joy of being with God forever in the kingdom of heaven. We see this, for example, in Psalm 16:11; Romans 15:13; Philippians 4:4; 1 Peter 1:8 and Revelation 19:7.

Old Testament joy

Deuteronomy
        12:6–7 ☐

1 Samuel 18:6 ☐

1 Kings 1:39–40 ☐

Simha and *sameah* are the usual Hebrew words for 'joy' and 'to rejoice'. They are expressed in celebration at the regular festivals and sacrifices – Deuteronomy 12:6–7; 1 Samuel 18:6 and 1 Kings 1:39–40.

Psalms 4:7 ☐
        42:4 ☐
        43:4 ☐
        81:1 ☐

Simha was not only expressed at pre-planned events, for the Book of Psalms shows that spontaneous joy was part of both corporate and individual worship – for example, Psalms 4:7; 42:4; 43:4 and 81:1.

Joy is a particular theme of the prophet Isaiah: he reveals that it is associated with the fullness of God's salvation and will be completed and fulfilled in the future – for example, Isaiah 49:13 and 61:10–11.

Isaiah 49:13 ☐
61:10–11 ☐

New Testament joy

Chara and *chairo* are the most usual Greek words for 'joy' and 'to rejoice'. They refer to 'intense joy' and are closely related to *charis* – which is the Greek word for 'grace'.

The relationship between *chara* and *charis* must suggest that *chara*, human joy, is the only appropriate response to *charis*, divine grace. John 15:11 and 16:22–24 establish that it is Jesus himself who communicates this joy, and that it is the result of our deep fellowship with him through his grace.

John 15:11 ☐
16:22–24 ☐

Acts 2:46; 8:8; 13:52 and 15:3 show that this intense joy characterises the life of the early church: for example, it accompanies the gift of the Spirit, the miracles performed in the name of Christ, the conversion of the Gentiles, and the celebration of the Lord's Supper.

Acts 2:46 ☐
8:8 ☐
13:52 ☐
15:3 ☐

In his letters, the apostle Paul teaches four basic facts about *chara*:

- *the conversion and Christian progress of new believers is a cause of joy* – Philippians 2:2; 1 Thessalonians 2:19–20

- *suffering for Christ's sake can lead to joy, because it is produced by the Lord and not by us* – 2 Corinthians 6:10; Colossians 1:24

- *it is a dynamic fruit of the Holy Spirit* – Galatians 5:22

- *every believer is called to share in the joy of Christ by fellowshipping with him and by practising rejoicing in the knowledge of him and his salvation* – Philippians 3:1; 4:4; 1 Thessalonians 5:16

Philippians 2:2 ☐
1 Thessalonians 2:19–20 ☐
2 Corinthians 6:10 ☐
Colossians 1:24 ☐
Galatians 5:22 ☐
Philippians 3:1 ☐
4:4 ☐
1 Thessalonians 5:16 ☐

Intense joy based in grace is so basic to the New Testament that it is easy to overlook the considerable variety of grounds and occasions for rejoicing which it describes. Christian believers are presented as rejoicing in, for example:

- *the Lord* – Philippians 3:1; 4:4

- *his incarnation* – Luke 1:14

- *his power* – Luke 13:17

Philippians 3:1 ☐
4:4 ☐
Luke 1:14 ☐
13:17 ☐

John 14:28 ☐
16:22 ☐
20:20 ☐
8:56 ☐
Acts 13:48 ☐
8:39 ☐
Luke 19:6 ☐
10:20 ☐
Acts 15:31 ☐
Romans 12:12 ☐
Matthew 5:12 ☐
Romans 16:19 ☐
Philippians 1:18 ☐
John 4:36 ☐
Acts 5:41 ☐
2 Corinthians
13:9 ☐
6:10 ☐
Acts 11:23 ☐
1 Corinthians
16:17 ☐
Philippians 4:10 ☐
Romans 12:15 ☐
2 Corinthians
7:16 ☐

- *his presence with the Father* – John 14:28

- *his presence with them* – John 16:22; 20:20

- *his ultimate triumph* – John 8:56

- *hearing the gospel* – Acts 13:48

- *their salvation* – Acts 8:39

- *receiving the Lord* – Luke 19:6

- *their enrolment in heaven* – Luke 10:20

- *their liberty in Christ* – Acts 15:31

- *their hope* – Romans 12:12

- *their reward* – Matthew 5:12

- *the obedience of other believers* – Romans 16:19

- *the proclamation of Christ* – Philippians 1:18

- *the gospel harvest* – John 4:36

- *suffering with Christ* – Acts 5:41

- *suffering in the cause of the gospel* – 2 Corinthians 13:9

- *suffering in persecution* – 2 Corinthians 6:10

- *the manifestation of grace* – Acts 11:23

- *meeting with other believers* – 1 Corinthians 16:17

- *receiving tokens of fellowship* – Philippians 4:10

- *the rejoicing of others* – Romans 12:15

- *learning of the well-being of others* – 2 Corinthians 7:16

When we are alert to the presence of intense joy and great rejoicing in the New Testament, we start to notice a spirit of joyous festivity which is not always evident in many sections of the church today.

But we will not enjoy a truly biblical life if our devoted service and our good doctrine are not leavened with times of intense celebration in the joy of the Lord.

THE SACRIFICE OF PRAISE

Nehemiah 8:10 is probably the best known verse about joy, and it shows that God's joy in us makes us strong. People cannot persevere with many things without joy. We can start almost anything with an act of our personal will, but we will not continue through difficulties and adversity without the experience or prospect of real joy.

Nehemiah 8:10 ☐

In this *Sword of the Spirit* series we often refer to 'gospel obedience' and contrast it with the obedience that God demanded under the Old Covenant. Without a spirit of joy, however, gospel obedience can become a lifeless device which is little different to the legal obedience of the Jewish Pharisees.

Our words and actions should be characterised by intense joy and great thanksgiving because our words and actions should be a response to God's gracious initiative. We speak and do only what we hear him say, and because our words and deeds come from the utterly self-consistent God, they come wrapped in his personal joy.

The way to joy

Although we can say that we are called to obey God with joy because of his grace, we can also say that joy comes by grace through obedience – that joy results from obedience.

In Luke 11:27–28, for example, Jesus taught that the people who live in obedience to God's word are more blessed than even the mother of the Son of God.

Luke 11:27–28 ☐

This is why the New Testament calls for the costly sacrifice of praise. We do not obtain joy easily by singing certain songs in a particular way; we obtain it through sacrifice, through gospel obedience.

We consider Jesus' Matthew 5:3–12 'beatitudes' in some detail in *The Rule of God*, and see that they involve a spiritual progression which climaxes in rejoicing and great gladness.

Matthew 5:3–12 ☐

Most older translations of the Bible render *makarios* as 'blessed' to stress that the quality comes from God. Many modern translations, however, render *makarios* as 'happy' because it suggests the idea of a 'large smile'.

Matthew
5:13–7:29 ☐

We need to grasp both these thoughts, for Jesus is saying that people will have *God-given* joyful smiles (and a matching inner heart attitude) when they live God's way. Jesus is calling for a state of joyous contentment in the beatitudes, and is showing that this results from hearing God's word *and* obeying it – from gospel obedience.

This means that we cannot know genuine joy until God has transformed the way we deal with the ordinary 'Sermon on the Mount' type events of life. If Matthew 5:13–7:29 is a series of examples of the beatitudes in action, it is also a description of a joy-producing life.

In public church worship today, some leaders seem almost to try to 'pump up' people with joy when nothing much has changed in their everyday lives – when they have not allowed God to break through into the routine of their daily lives. But godly celebration which is 'in spirit and truth' can spring only from lives which have been transformed by God and are being renewed by his Holy Spirit.

Continuous rejoicing

Philippians
4:4–20 ☐

In Philippians 4:4–20, the apostle Paul teaches about rejoicing.

- *he instructs us to rejoice continuously in the Lord* – verse 4

- *he associates rejoicing with gentleness* – verse 5

- *he presents the two aspects of rejoicing: be anxious for nothing; and make requests to God with thanksgiving* – verse 6

- *he sets out the results of rejoicing; the personal peace of God will guard our hearts and minds through Christ Jesus* – verse 7

In this important passage, Paul teaches how we can rejoice continuously – and his first instruction is to be full of care for nothing.

Matthew 6:25 ☐

Leviticus 25:21 ☐

Jesus gave much the same advice in Matthew 6:25, and it clearly follows on from the Leviticus 25:21 promise that God will provide for the jubilee so that the year-long rejoicing can be founded on a freedom from worry and care.

We will not be able to rejoice 'in spirit and in truth' until we have learned to be anxious for nothing. And we will not have a carefree indifference to things until we have learnt to trust God completely.

In the Old Testament, it simply was not possible for anyone to celebrate the jubilee unless they deeply trusted God's ability and will to provide enough for their needs. So too in the age of the perpetual jubilee of the spirit, we will not be able to rejoice continuously in the Lord unless we rely entirely on God to provide what we need.

But Paul does not stop at verse 7. He carries on to instruct us to set our minds on *all* the things in life which are noble, just, pure, lovely, virtuous and praiseworthy. Just as God rejoiced and took pleasure in his creation, so too we should focus on everything in life which is good. This is another divinely appointed way to the joy of the Lord.

Too many believers think that they will have joy only by praying and singing. But these are expressions of joy rather than the exclusive way to joy. If we trust God completely, and fill our lives with the simple and lovely things of God's creation, we will know joy. The promise is absolute.

This is why praise is a sacrifice, and why worship is service. Our will is deeply involved in gospel obedience, in trusting God completely, and in setting our minds on noble, lovely things. It is a consciously chosen way of thinking and doing – but it is not a way of self effort.

As we see throughout this series in every area of the Spirit, when we respond to the Father's gracious initiative with faith, his healing reaches into the inner recesses of our lives to develop our faith and strengthen our trust – joy in-and-from the Lord is the inevitable result.

EXPRESSIONS OF REJOICING

Jesus rejoiced so fully in life that the religious leaders of his day accused him of being a glutton and a drunkard. Sadly, there have always been people in the church who are more concerned with what they call 'reverence' than with what the Bible calls rejoicing.

The 'careless' followers of Christ should be the most free, the most alive, the most interesting, and the most stimulating of men and women. Rejoicing adds festivity to our serving to make us truly complete people who really are living in the image of our rejoicing, foot-washing God.

We have seen in Parts Three and Four how the Old Testament people of God praised him with music and hymns, with shouts and dancing, with choirs and prophetic songs, with festivals and celebrations, with giving and hospitality, in the temple and the family home.

We have much to learn from the rich variety of their praise. But we must recognise that these are examples of rejoicing rather than biblically required forms.

Acts 10 □

We need to learn, like Peter in Acts 10, that nothing which comes from the gracious hand of God is unclean; and we need to realise that we are free to celebrate the grace and goodness of God with every type of art and handiwork, with every aspect of our being, and in ways which are particularly relevant to our own age and culture.

Although we cannot manufacture spontaneous joy, we can make regular family events – like, for example, birthdays – into special times of celebration. And although festivals which are based in the agricultural year – like Rogation and Harvest – may not be relevant for urban churches, we can redeem the other festivals of our own culture and use them creatively as occasions of genuine celebration.

For example, instead of complaining about Halloween, we could fill our churches and homes with lights and celebrate Christ's victory over darkness. Furthermore, as the evening of October 31st is the traditional time for remembering the saints who have gone before, we can celebrate the lives of believers whom God has greatly used in our church and tradition, and can pass on their stories to new generations of believers.

We can reclaim the great Christian festivals like Christmas, Easter, Ascension Day and Pentecost, and turn them into special times of godly celebration. We can make special occasions when we celebrate Christ's return and the Bible, overseas missions and the work of God in a different part of our own country. And those who live in multi-racial communities can learn to enjoy the cuisine, music, dancing and art forms of other cultures.

God's people in the Old Testament had at least seven great festivals in each year, and some of these lasted for several days. As we have seen, they focused on different aspects of God's dealing with the nation and were times of feasting and rejoicing, of music and shouting, of repentance and fresh commitment, of genuine community life.

Above all, the Old Testament festivals enabled God's people to draw back from their domestic lives and to understand and experience their essential nationhood.

There is a godly principle in these events: even though, in Christ, we have been redeemed from the Old Testament rules about the Sabbath, we still need to live by the deeper Sabbath principle of regular rest from work; in the same way, although Christ has fulfilled all the Old Testament festivals, we still need to make room for festivals in our lives so that we can appreciate and enjoy the nationhood of the church and the oneness of the body.

The joy of the Lord is our strength, and celebratory events seem to provide us with a boost which enables us to persevere through the more mundane periods of the year. This is God's pattern of life, for he has created a world full of seasons, with times of warmth and cold, dormancy and growth, blossom and harvest, night and day, and so on.

Rejoicing in the Lord gives us the strength to serve others, it provides us with the inspiration to worship him in the ordinary detail of our lives, and it equips us with the joy to give generously to the needy and to God's work.

When we start to fill our lives with godly service, godly giving and godly rejoicing, we will be people who are beginning to be the worshippers whom the Father is seeking – we will be worshipping him in spirit and truth.

PART NINE

the holy spirit and worship

In *Glory in the Church*, we see that worship is the supreme, all-embracing call of the whole Christian church. Before everything else, the universal church (and every local expression) is called to be a worshipping community. If worship in spirit and truth is not central to every congregation, all other activities must be out of line.

In Philippians 3:3, the apostle Paul teaches that we worship God 'by the Spirit of God'. A few English versions of the Bible translate this as 'in the Spirit', but it makes little difference – both prepositions show that true worship depends entirely on the Holy Spirit.

Without the help of the Spirit, we cannot offer one acceptable word or deed of worship to the Father. As we see in *Knowing the Spirit*, it is he who inspires our praise and prayers, leads us into the truth, convicts us of our sin, and gives us gifts to help us worship/serve God.

Paul's greatest chapters about public worship, 1 Corinthians 11–14, are dominated by the Greek verb *oikodomeo*. This literally means 'to build a house', but is usually translated as 'to edify'. 1 Corinthians 14:26 suggests that every aspect of the church's worship should build together the members of the body and so build up the church.

Philippians 3:3 ☐

1 Corinthians
14:26 ☐

Throughout this book, we have seen that worship is more than singing hymns and speaking prayers. Worship/service is our total response to God's initiative, and includes the way that we offer the sacrifice of our bodies in selfless service, the sacrifice of our possessions in giving and hospitality, and the sacrifice of our praise in constant rejoicing. All these sacrifices of worship/service must be made in-or-by the Spirit *and* they must build the church of Christ.

In a worthy attempt to keep things simple and easily understood, some leaders try to keep these two aspects of worship apart. They teach how the Spirit directs our worship, and – quite separately – they teach how our worship should build the church.

This approach, however, can suggest that these two aspects of worship are unrelated. But the Spirit works in many complementary ways with the express purpose of shaping a church which offers worship that is both acceptable to God *and* edifying to his church. This means that the Spirit's role in worship is more than inspiring a song and creating an atmosphere of his presence, he is also always moulding us together in love.

THE SPIRIT CREATES UNITY

Psalm 133 □

Psalm 133 is a wonderful prophetic Psalm about God's people and the unity of the Spirit. It describes the moral rightness and emotional pleasure of unity, links it to the anointing oil of the Spirit and the heavenly dew of the Spirit, and shows that this unity of the Spirit is blessed by God with eternal life.

Psalm 133 is the penultimate 'Song of Ascents', and many scholars believe that it may have been sung by Old Testament pilgrims at the end of their journey – when they were approaching the Jerusalem temple to worship their God with sacrifice at a time of festival.

The pilgrims left their homes and villages in ones and twos, and gathered together into a larger group as they met with others along the way. According to popular tradition, this Psalm was sung to celebrate the oneness that they had discovered and enjoyed in God, and in their common purpose of preparing to enjoy one of the great festivals.

Psalm 133 points to the important truth that we set out to God on our own, in personal faith, and that our move towards worship is an act of our individual will. It also shows, however, that God has bigger plans, and that he works to build us together with others so that we offer him *corporate worship* which is based in Spirit-made oneness.

The apostle Paul does not refer to Psalm 133 in Ephesians 4:1–16, but he teaches the same truth. He explains that the Spirit creates 'unity in diversity' and that it is the job of believers to maintain this unity and not spoil it. Like so much in the Christian life, unity is entirely a grace-gift of God, but we have to work hard at using and developing it.

Ephesians 4:1–16 ☐

It is almost impossible to over-emphasise this work of the Spirit, for it is one of the great themes of the New Testament, and it accounts for so much in the life and teaching of the early church. For example:

- *there is no room in the one body for distinctions of race, gender, class or education* – Colossians 3:11; James 2:1–4

  Colossians 3:11 ☐
  James 2:1–4 ☐

- *the natural gaps and hostility between races, classes and cultures must be broken down* – Ephesians 2:15

  Ephesians 2:15 ☐

- *there is no place for boasting or personal pride as everything is a gift from God* – 1 Corinthians 4:7

  1 Corinthians 4:7 ☐

- *every effort must be made to maintain unity and communication between different groups of believers* – Acts 8; 15; 18:21; 20:16; Romans 15:26; 1 Corinthians 16:1; 2 Corinthians 8–9

  Acts 8 ☐
  15 ☐
  18:21 ☐
  20:16 ☐
  Romans 15:26 ☐
  1 Corinthians 16:1 ☐
  2 Corinthians 8–9 ☐

- *believers must stand together and serve together* – Philippians 1:27; 2:1–2; 4:1–3

  Philippians 1:27 ☐
  2:1–2 ☐
  4:1–3 ☐

- *no believer or group of believers has special knowledge* – Colossians 1:26–28; 1 John 2:20, 27

  Colossians 1:26–28 ☐
  1 John 2:20, 27 ☐

Unity at Antioch

The church at Antioch is a shining example of Spirit-made unity. Acts 13:1–2 shows that the leadership was corporate, that it included prophets and teachers, and that it was made up of a remarkable mixture of men. For example:

Acts 13:1–2 ☐

- *Barnabas was a rich, land-owning Cypriot levite*

- *Simeon was a Black African*

- *Lucius was a Jew from the dispersion in North Africa*

- *Manaen was educated at the court of king Herod*

- *Saul/Paul was a Pharisee who had studied under Gamaliel*

This group of leaders demonstrates the sort of unity that the Spirit creates. Christ's John 17:21 will for his church was being so obviously fulfilled and developed in this mixed community of believers that they were the first people to be given the name 'Christians'.

John 17:21 ☐

Antioch was Paul's first experience of Christian leadership, and it seems to have shaped and envisioned his thinking about oneness. It explains why he was so angry and distressed when he heard about the divisions in the church at Corinth – he knew that it should be different and he knew that it could be different.

Disunity at Corinth

The first three chapters of Paul's first letter to the church at Corinth are dominated by the practical problem of unity. It seems that the believers in Corinth were thinking about their faith mainly in an intellectual manner, and that they imagined themselves to be judges between the various emphases of the wider church leaders.

1 Corinthians 1–3 ☐

In 1 Corinthians 1–3, Paul insists that the gospel is not like philosophical wisdom, and that its teachers are not travelling intellectuals; rather, they are co-operating workers in God's vineyard – one plants, another waters, but God alone makes things grow.

In these chapters, Paul makes a series of important points which underline the relationship between Spirit-created unity and the church as essentially a worshipping community.

- *the church cannot allow division any more than Christ can – 1:13*

- *God has built the church into a temple for the Spirit to indwell – 3:16*

- *anyone who spoils the temple of God by encouraging disunity will be destroyed by God – 3:17*

By identifying the church as the new temple, Paul implies that the church is made for worship and is made to be filled with God's presence. Just as the old temple was set apart for the worship of God and was filled with God's glory at the hour of sacrifice, so the new temple of the church is being built for worship and to be the community which reveals God's glorious presence in-and-to the world.

1 Peter 2:5 develops 'the temple' metaphor, and we consider it more fully in *Glory in the Church*.

1 Peter 2:5 ☐

In a similar way, Jesus' prayer for unity, in John 17, was offered in the context of worship – at the feast of Passover, immediately after he had instituted the Lord's Supper and introduced the work of the Holy Spirit. And Paul's plea for unity, in 1 Corinthians 1–3, prepares the ground for his teaching about public worship, the Lord's Supper and the work of the Holy Spirit in worship.

John 17 ☐

Unless we recognise God's desire to move us on from our starting point of personal worship to our destiny of corporate worship (and we co-operate with his will in this), and unless we appreciate the supreme importance of the work of the Spirit in relation to unity (and we do our utmost to maintain and develop what he has made), all our attempts at Spirit-inspired worship are likely to be in vain.

He brings fellowship

The Spirit not only creates unity, he also creates *koinonia*, fellowship or communion – which is the principle practical expression of unity.

We consider this more fully in *Glory in the Church* – where we see that biblical 'fellowship' or 'communion' literally means 'sharing', and that it involves 'having a share in something', 'giving a share in something', and 'sharing in something with someone'.

2 Corinthians 13:14 and Philippians 2:1 mention 'the *koinonia* of the Spirit'. This could mean 'the sharing which the Spirit gives' or 'sharing in the Spirit': these two interpretations are not far apart, for the Spirit gives a share of himself to every believer. The fellowship we enjoy with other believers, therefore, is based in our mutual sharing in the Holy Spirit.

2 Corinthians
13:14 ☐

Philippians 2:1 ☐

Acts 2:42–47 and 4:32–37 are the best biblical illustrations of this Spirit-created sharing. The new believers devoted themselves to 'fellowship', and this manifested itself to such an extent in the sacrifice of their possessions and in the sacrifice of constant rejoicing that large numbers of people were attracted to the faith.

Acts 2:42–47 ☐
4:32–37 ☐

Acts 11:27–30 ☐

We can say that the way the believers expressed their fellowship affected the way they worshipped *and* that it built the church up. We see much the same expression of sharing in Acts 11:27–30.

THE SPIRIT ENABLES WORSHIP

Acts 2:47 ☐
    3:8–9 ☐

The book of Acts shows that the Spirit led the first believers to a tremendous depth of worship. They celebrated the Lord's Supper in their homes; they ate together with great joy; and they were characterised by their praise of God – even when they were threatened or imprisoned. Acts 2:47 and 3:8–9 show that praise and worship was a special and immediate result of the Spirit's work in their lives.

As we have seen in Part Five, the believers participated in formal temple worship, informal home meetings, regular synagogue services and in organised open-air gatherings for prayer.

Whenever Acts describes the believers arranging their own worship (after the split from Judaism), it invariably mentions the Holy Spirit.

Acts 4:23–31 ☐

Psalm 2 ☐

Acts 4:23–31, for example, records how the church (when Peter and John had returned with the Council's instructions) immediately gave themselves to prayer rather than to protest or practical action. They based their prayers around Psalm 2, and the Holy Spirit manifested himself in unusual power while they prayed and worshipped God.

Acts 13:1–3 ☐

And in Acts 13:1–3, before the first missionary journey, the Antioch church was united in worship and was demonstrating their seriousness by fasting. It was within this context that the Spirit revealed his leading and called Barnabas and Paul to service. Once again, we see the biblical principle that practical service *flows from* spiritual worship.

1 Corinthians
    14:25 ☐

It is the same in Paul's letters. For example, he makes it clear in 1 Corinthians 14:25 that visitors to public church worship (where the members are open to the Spirit and are allowing him to speak through them) will be conscious that God is present and moved to worship.

Revelation 1:4 ☐

We can also say that the book of Revelation springs from John being in the Spirit on the Lord's day – doubtless in the context of worship.

He inspires Scripture

The Spirit's inspiration of the Scriptures is very closely associated with his enabling of worship.

As we have seen throughout this *Sword of the Spirit* series, the Old Testament prophets claimed to have been sent and inspired by the Spirit of God. Jesus endorsed the Spirit's inspiration of Psalm 110 in Mark 12:36; and Acts 1:16; 4:25 and 2 Timothy 3:16 plainly attribute the Old Testament to work of the Spirit.

Psalm 110 ☐

Mark 12:36 ☐

Acts 1:16 ☐

4:25 ☐

2 Timothy 3:16 ☐

1 Peter 1:10–12 ☐

2 Peter 1:20–21 ☐

1 Peter 1:10–12 and 2 Peter 1:20–21 are the clearest biblical explanations of the process of inspiration. 2 Peter 1:20–21 uses a Greek metaphor which suggests the way that a sailing ship is carried along by the wind. The prophets raised their 'sails' to the Holy Spirit – they were attentive, receptive and obedient – and he filled them and carried them along in the direction that he chose.

This is classic example of the sort of partnership with the Spirit that we stress in *Knowing the Spirit*. The Spirit co-operated with anointed men and women who were yielded to him. He did not repress their personalities and backgrounds and use them as mere dictation machines; instead, he whispered his thoughts into their spirits and they passed these on in their distinctive styles.

The first believers, however, did not only look back to the way that the Spirit had inspired Scripture in the past, and use only the fruit of his past inspiration in their praise and worship. They also knew that Jesus had promised the Spirit to them, that he had promised the Spirit would teach them and lead them into all truth, and they knew that the Spirit had been directing them since Pentecost.

It followed, therefore, that the Spirit who had inspired the prophets to point forward to Jesus was also inspiring them as they bore witness to Jesus. This is Peter's main point in 1 Peter 1:10–12, and explains why he sets Paul's letters alongside the Old Testament in 2 Peter 3:16.

2 Peter 3:16 ☐

1 Corinthians 2:13–16 ☐

14:38 ☐

Colossians 4:16 ☐

1 Thessalonians 2:13 ☐

It is also why Paul claimed to have the mind of Christ, to proclaim the word of God, to teach details given by the Spirit, and to ask for his letters to be read aloud in public worship – 1 Corinthians 2:13–16; 14:38; Colossians 4:16 and 1 Thessalonians 2:13.

As we see in *Living Faith* and *Listening to God*, the Scriptures are central to every area of life and faith, and this is why Bible reading has always been a key feature of private and public worship in the church.

Some people accuse Protestant Christians of almost worshipping the Bible. We do not turn to the Scriptures, however, to worship them; we turn to them because the Spirit who inspired them is to be encountered in them. We read them to hear from him and to be transformed by him into the likeness of Christ – as Paul explains in 2 Corinthians 3:1–18.

2 Corinthians 3:1–18 □

THE SPIRIT BUILDS UP THE CHURCH

It seems that the church in Corinth was a talented and gifted community. It was vital, dynamic, free, open, confident and fresh – and yet it was also in serious danger.

From Paul's first letter to them, it seems that there were making two mistakes. They appear to have believed that extraordinary, uncontrolled 'ecstatic' manifestations were the hallmark of the Spirit's presence. And they seem to have valued the people who spoke in tongues more highly than those who prophesied and taught.

By supposing that ecstasy – losing self-control – was a sure sign of divine inspiration, they were denying the rationality, the personality and the morality of the Holy Spirit. They were forgetting that he was the Spirit of Jesus who was always perfectly under control.

This emphasis on ecstatic manifestations seems to have led the Corinthians to conclude that it did not matter how they behaved so long as this supposed mark of divine inspiration was upon them. It also appears to have led to excessive 'individualism' (those who did not have a gift were jealous, and those who did were proud), and to have damaged interdependence and caused competition and division.

In his first letter to the Corinthian church, after dealing with issues about division and unity, with the practical problems they were facing in worship, and with the Lord's Supper, Paul deals with this problem in 1 Corinthians 12.

1 Corinthians 12 □

1 Corinthians 12

First, Paul reminds them that ecstatic speech is *not* Christian in origin. They had been 'carried away' before their conversion when they worshipped false gods and shared in pagan feasts. It is possible that Paul's use of *apagomenoi* in 12:2 means that they had experienced demonic possession, and had been taken 'out of themselves' in ecstatic speech as they worshipped idols which were dumb.

It is not easy to understand what Paul means in 12:3. He could be contrasting Spirit-inspired praise in church services with demonic-inspired cries at pagan altars. Or he could mean that someone had cried 'Jesus is accursed' in a Corinthian church service, and that this had been accepted as being inspired by the Spirit. No matter where this cry was uttered, Paul uses it to teach an important lesson.

The crucial mark of the Spirit's presence in worship is the confession that 'Jesus is Lord'. This shows that the basic test of every claim to the Spirit's inspiration is whether or not the content of the proclamation is Christ-centred and Christ-honouring. In this, Paul is simply repeating the same points that he stressed in chapters 3–4 – that the Spirit bears witness to the historical Jesus who is the Lord of the whole universe, and that the hallmark of the Spirit's presence is an unambiguous declaration of Jesus' absolute lordship.

In 1 Corinthians 12:4–6, Paul contrasts the variety of gifts with the unity of the Giver. He shows that one God acts in three different ways.

- *charismata*, gifts of grace, are linked with the Holy Spirit

- *diakonia*, acts of lowly service, are associated with Jesus the Son

- *energema*, the necessary empowering, comes from God the Father

This proves that the spiritual gifts we receive are given by the supreme Gift of grace: they are not possessions to use as we please, and they are not rewards for good behaviour; instead, they are tools which are intended for *diakonia*, for the service of others after the pattern of the one who was anointed with the Spirit without limit and was the foot-washing Servant of God.

And when this service is effective, when it helps others, heals them, builds them up, it is not due to our holiness or talent, it is due *only* to the empowering given by God the Father.

In verses 7–11, Paul develops his argument by telling the Corinthians that the Spirit gives different gifts to *every* member of the church, and that although these gifts have different manifestations, they are all for the common good. We consider these spiritual gifts in detail in *Knowing the Spirit* and *Ministry in the Spirit*.

In these verses, Paul lays down a second and complementary truth about the criteria by which we can discern the work of the Spirit.

In verse 3, he shows that we must ask:

- *does the proclamation point unmistakably to Jesus as Lord?*

And in verse 7 he reveals that we must also ask:

- *does the manifestation benefit and build the church?*

It is imperative we grasp that the content of the proclamation and the results in the community of God's people are the two most important tests and measures of people's words, claims, experience and activity.

In these crucial verses, Paul establishes that the unity of the Spirit works through a variety of gifts, and he bases this in the nature and work of God. Because God is himself 'unity-in-diversity' (we consider this in *Knowing the Father*), and has revealed himself this way through all his creating and saving acts in history, so the church inevitably expresses his divine 'unity-in-diversity' when he is present and active.

One God is the source of all the different manifestations of the One Spirit in the body of the One Son. These manifestations are called *energemata* when the emphasis is on what God does by his power – as in verses 6 and 10; they are called *charismata* when the emphasis is on the gracious gift of his sovereign distribution – as in verses 4, 9 and 28; and they are called *diakonia* to remind us that all gifts and empowerings of God are intended for the service of others.

The body

From verse 12 to the end of the chapter, Paul uses the metaphor of the church as 'Christ's body' to develop the purpose of the Spirit's gifts.

It is God the Father who appoints us to our place in the body of Christ and gives us the gifts we need to carry out our appointed function – verses 18, 24 and 28. And it is the Holy Spirit who actually makes us members of the body – verse 13.

Paul insists that all believers have been baptised in one Spirit into the one body: some may have more impressive gifts than others, but all have been immersed in the Holy Spirit and all have had him poured into their lives.

Verse 12 is especially important. Paul does not say that, just as the body is one and has many members, and all the members of the body, though many, are one body, so it is *with the church*. Instead, he says, so it is *with Christ*.

The church is not a human society, it is the embodiment of Jesus. Whatever the church is, whatever it does, it is and does by the power, the presence and the activity of Jesus. He is the one in whom all believers are incorporated, and this is why Paul's favourite description of believers is 'in Christ'.

Paul is explaining to the Corinthians that, if believers are different, it is because Christ is in them and they are in Christ, and that they do not belong to the church but rather to Christ. He is showing them that their divisive spirit is not so much affecting the harmony of the church as affecting Christ personally.

Paul then deals with two common tendencies within the body of Christ. In verses 14–20, Paul encourages those who feel that they are *inferior* members of the body, and explains that all members are interdependent and equally important.

And in verses 21–26 he corrects those who suffer from a *superiority* complex. If they look down on the members with less spectacular gifts and functions, the whole body is impoverished.

Throughout this chapter, Paul's main thrust is to teach the Corinthians that the whole church loses when all the members do not get the chance to make their God-given contribution to the worship and service of the church. The Corinthians had to learn that they were not individual 'Christs' with all the gifts, but joint-members of Christ with some gifts. No believer is unnecessary and no believer is self-sufficient; we all need each other in the body of Christ.

Love

It is at this point that Paul writes about a more excellent way, about *agape* love.

According to Paul, love is the greatest gift that the Spirit can give to enhance the church's worship and build the church, and all his other valuable gifts – tongues, prophecy, miracles, knowledge, wisdom, miracles, and so on – can function effectively only through this love.

1 Corinthians 13 ☐

Romans 5:5 ☐

The love that Paul describes in 1 Corinthians 13 cannot be worked up by human effort, it can come only from the Holy Spirit. This is also Paul's emphasis in Romans 5:5.

Every gift of the Spirit is important for worship and service, but there can be no higher gift for worship and service than the love which Paul describes in 1 Corinthians 13 – this is why it comes in the midst of his teaching about the gifts of the Holy Spirit. Unless people meet the living, loving Christ through a believer, it is irrelevant whether they have prophetic insight, miraculous power or pray in tongues.

We may worship regularly, celebrate creatively, sacrifice our possessions, serve humbly and praise enthusiastically, but we will achieve nothing of any lasting value unless the selfless *agape* love of Jesus motivates and fills us, and directs all our worship/service.

In this beautiful chapter, Paul contrasts the love of Jesus with the shortcomings of the church in Corinth. He shows that Jesus' love is the opposite of the Corinthians':

- *pride in spiritual experience which puffed them up* – verse 4

- *emphasis on particular gifts which made them feel either proud or jealous* – verse 4

- *selfish exercise of special gifts for personal gratification which Paul calls 'seeking one's own'* – verse 5

The Corinthians were seeking what they thought was the higher way of spiritual experience, but Paul set an even better way before them – the love of Jesus the Servant who was never puffed up and who was never selfish in the exercise of his gifts. Everything about Jesus was always for God and always for others.

Throughout this *Sword of the Spirit* series, we have consistently seen that a loving self-giving in worship and service is the way of Jesus, the way of the Spirit and – as Paul shows in verses 10–13 – it is the way of the church in heaven.

When all prophecy has been fulfilled and all earthly gifts completed, when faith has become sight and hope has become experience, only *agape* love will still remain. On 'the Last Day', the eternal, universal body of Christ will finally be fully united in adoring worship and devoted love – perfect worship and service in spirit and truth will finally begin, and it will never cease.

HEAVENLY WORSHIP

Throughout this book, we have seen that true worship is God's eternal heart for all sinful people. Since the dawn of time, the Father has been actively seeking sinful men and women who will be his people and will worship him in spirit and truth.

Even now, he is drawing believers together essentially to worship him, and is still gently persuading us that this is his good-and-perfect will for our lives.

We have considered the insights of Proverbs 8, which seems to show that God has been rejoicing in-and-with himself for all eternity – even before his worship overflowed into creation. This seems to suggest that all creation was made primarily to join in with the pre-existing heavenly worship, and so to enjoy God in his presence forever.

The Scriptures include several other insights which also appear to show that heaven is characterised by true worship and great rejoicing. For example:

- *Isaiah 6:1–3 describes the angelic rejoicing which goes on within heaven*

  Isaiah 6:1–3 ☐

- *Ezekiel 40–47 suggests that heavenly worship is the destiny of God's people*

  Ezekiel 40–47 ☐

- *Luke 2:13–14 reveals the great praise of the heavenly host*

  Luke 2:13–14 ☐

- *Luke 15:7 and 10 show that there is rejoicing in heaven*

  15:7, 10 ☐

These insights, however, are dwarfed by the awesome descriptions in the book of Revelation, which make God's ultimate purposes plain. He is drawing us together to a place of total worship, where we will live together in his perfect presence forever, and will spend eternity rejoicing together in-and-with him.

Worship in Revelation

Heavenly worship is the backdrop and context for all the visions of the book of Revelation. We must take care that we are not so concerned to understand the apostle John's visions correctly that we overlook what he reveals about the place and priority of heavenly worship.

Revelation 4 ☐
        5:8–14 ☐
        7:9–17 ☐
      11:15–19 ☐
        15:3–5 ☐
          16:5 ☐

Revelation 4 is the first of John's descriptions of heavenly worship: verse 2 shows that this recognition and appreciation of worship can come only in-and-through the Spirit, and verses 8–11 reveal that everything in heaven lives to worship God. It is much the same in 5:8–14; 7:9–17; 11:15–19 and 15:3–5.

These important passages show that heavenly worship embraces ancient hymns (15:3) and brand new songs (5:9); that it focuses entirely on the person of God (4:8, 11; 5:9, 13; 7:12; 11:17; 15:3; 16:5); and that it celebrates what God has done, what he is doing, and what he has promised to do (4:11; 5:9–10, 12, 13; 11:17–18; 15:4).

In particular, the book of Revelation reveals that heavenly worship revolves around two great themes of worship:

- *the song of creation* – Revelation 4:11

- *the song of salvation* – Revelation 5:9

These two themes appear constantly throughout Scripture, and both reveal everything about God's person and character – his power and his love, his grace and his purity, and so on. Because God reveals himself through his mighty acts, we experience him for who he is when we worship him in his presence as Creator and Saviour.

As *creation* is the essential overflow of God's own worship, the worship of God as creator has always been at the heart of worship. Creation is a visible evidence of God's power and might, and a proof of his uniqueness and supremacy. Through creation, the Old Testament people of God were able to recognise that God was the only God, and that other gods were simply impotent idols.

The Jews were called to worship one God because they knew through creation that there was only one God, and this was meant to determine how they lived and served. Many Psalms celebrate God as creator, and his handiwork of creation and divine creativity – seen again in the new heaven and earth – is a major theme of heavenly worship.

Many modern believers fail to sing the song of creation, and neglect to worship God as creator. In their worship, they focus almost entirely upon God's work of salvation. But the Father's work of redemption is inseparably linked with his work of creation (he has the right to redeem only because it is his creation) and we cannot appreciate redemption properly without recognising its vital link with creation. We consider this in *Knowing the Father*.

In the Old Testament, the people of Israel knew that God continually acted to save them from their enemies, from famine, from disease, and so on. They knew that *Yahweh* was their Saviour, and that their existence as a nation depended upon his mighty acts of deliverance. In particular, their deliverance from slavery in Egypt was basic to their understanding of God, and 'the song of Moses' in Exodus 15:1–21 was their definitive expression of worship to God as Saviour – this is the hymn which Revelation shows is still being sung in heaven.

Exodus 15:1–21 ☐

We know, however, that God has performed an even greater act of salvation for his people than the passover miracle. At the cross, Jesus became the Saviour of the whole world, delivered us all from the slavery of sin, and decisively defeated our enemy. This has become the theme of countless songs of salvation sung through the ages, and is the theme of the new heavenly songs of Revelation 1:5–6 and 5:9–14.

Revelation 1:5–6 ☐
5:9–14 ☐

Personal and corporate

Revelation's most telling insight into heavenly worship is its consistent presentation of heavenly worshippers as being both fully individual and completely corporate.

Revelation 5:11–13, for example, reports that 'ten thousand times ten thousand, and thousands and thousands' and 'every creature in heaven and on the earth and under the earth' are united in one expression of worship. They retain their distinctive personhood but have been brought by the Spirit to a climax of worshipping oneness.

It is the same in Revelation 7:9–10, which records how 'a great multitude which no one could number, of all nations, tribes, people and tongue' are standing before the throne and shouting praise to God. Their individual, national, tribal and linguistic differences are still obvious, but they are united in praise and worship to God. They are offering praise and worship which is personal to them, but which is expressed through their Spirit-made corporate oneness.

Revelation 7:9–10 ☐

This, then, is our destiny – to be an eternal worshipper who is thoroughly personal yet fully united with all other worshippers.

Like the people of Israel in the days of the first temple, we have been drawn by God's grace towards him. In faith, we have set out on a personal pilgrimage towards him, and have then discovered that God is building us together with the other believers in our area.

Together with them, we are journeying on towards him, learning to worship and serve together, beginning to appreciate our interdependence in the body, struggling at times with the tensions but working to maintain the unity of the Spirit.

And the great goal of eternal, heavenly worship in the intimate presence of God is always before us. It has always been God's greatest desire for us to enjoy him in the same way, and just as intensely, as we read the persons of God rejoiced in themselves in Proverbs 8.

The God who is personal but corporate, one but more than one, is drawing us into exactly the same eternal enjoyment of personal but corporate rejoicing. In his great grace and mercy, the Father is seeking yet more sinful men and women who will worship him in spirit and truth, and will enjoy his glorious presence forever.

ACTIVITIES for individuals and small groups

the father's priority

What do Jesus' words in John 4:21–24 reveal to you about God's heart?

....

....

What do Jesus' words in John 4:21–24 reveal to you about worship?

....

....

Why did Jesus bring this revelation about God to a sinful, female, non-Jew rather than to his disciples?

....

....

....

List some biblical examples of the Father taking the initiative in his dealings with humanity.

....

....

....

What is worship in spirit? How can you worship God in spirit?

....

....

....

What does Matthew 4:10 teach you about worship?

....

....

What does Exodus 20:3–5 teach you about worship?

....

....

....

How can you worship God in truth?

....

....

....

What does Isaiah 6:5 teach you about worship? What is your personal experience of this?

....

....

....

....

....

What do Jesus' words in Mark 12:28–34 teach about worshipping God and serving others?

....

....

....

If someone examined your life, which of 'serving others' and 'worshipping God' would they assume was your higher priority? Why is this?

....

....

....

If your worship is a response to God's initiative, what should you expect to happen when you worship?

....

....

....

Why is God calling you to worship him?

....

....

....

....

THE LEADER OF WORSHIP

What important principle of worship does Exodus 10:24–26 establish?

....

....

....

....

What does this mean practically for you in your personal, private worship/service?

....

....

....

....

What does it mean practically for the public worship in your local church?

....

....

....

....

How can the different aspects of public church worship reveal that God is the only initiator and the ultimate leader of worship?

....

....

....

....

If God is directing and leading the public worship, what can you expect to experience when you worship?

....

....

....

....

OUR RESPONSE

How did worship effect God's people in the Old Testament?

....
....
....

What does Isaiah 6:8 teach you about the human results of worship?

....
....
....

List some other biblical examples of worship leading to obedient service?

....
....
....

How, specifically, has God recently directed you during worship?

....
....
....

How did you respond to this prompting?

....
....
....

Describe the spiritual progression involved in worship in spirit and truth.

....
....
....
....

praise and worship

Many people believe that 'worship' means one thing and that 'service' means something different. They assume that 'worship' means spiritual activities like singing and praying, and that 'service' means practical actions like sweeping floors and arranging chairs. The Bible, however, makes no such distinction. As far as the Scriptures are concerned, our worship of God is our service of God; the way that we serve him is the way that we worship him.

The following passages all use the same Hebrew word 'abodah'. What do they teach about the relationship between worship and service?

Exodus 3:12; 7:16; 8:1, 20; 9:1, 13; 23:25; Deuteronomy 10:12; 11:13; Joshua 24:14–16; Psalm 2:11; 100:2; Jeremiah 30:9; Zephaniah 3:9

....

....

Exodus 36:1–5; Numbers 3:7–8; 4:23–28, 47–49; 1 Chronicles 28:20–21; 2 Chronicles 24:12

....

....

....

Exodus 12:25–26; Numbers 8:11, 19–26; 18:6–7; 1 Chronicles 23:24–32; 25:1–8; 2 Chronicles 35:1–19

....

....

....

The same Greek word 'latreia' is used in all these passages. What do they teach about biblical worship/service?

Matthew 4:10; Luke 1:74; 2:37; 4:8; Acts 7:7; 24:14; 26:7; 27:23; Romans 1:9; 9:4; 12:1; Philippians 3:3; 2 Timothy 1:3; Hebrews 8:5; 9:1, 6, 14; 10:2; 12:28; Revelation 7:15 and 22:3

....

....

....

....

BOWING DOWN

While the words *abodah* and *latreia* emphasise the relationship between worship and service, the words *shachah* and *proskuneo* stress that the essence of worship/service is bowing down before God.

All these passages use 'shachah'; what do they teach you about worship?

Genesis 22:5; 24:26–28; Exodus 4:31; 12:27; 24:1; 34:8; Deuteronomy 26:10; 1 Samuel 1:28; 1 Chronicles 16:29; 29:20; 2 Chronicles 20:18; 29:30; Nehemiah 8:6; 9:3; Job 1:20; Psalm 95:6; 96:9; 99:5.

....

....

....

....

....

All these passages use 'proskuneo'; what do they teach you about worship?

Matthew 2:11; 4:9; 8:2; 9:18; 14:33; 15:25; 18:26; 28:9; Mark 5:6; 15:19; John 4:23–24; 9:38; Acts 10:25; 24:11; 1 Corinthians 14:25; Revelation 4:10; 7:11; 11:16; 19:4, 10 and 22:8.

....

....

....

....

....

When God calls you to worship him, what is he principally looking for?

....

....

....

....

What does John 4:1–24 teach about outward and inward aspects of worship?

....

....

....

PRAISE

The Bible uses several Greek and Hebrew words to show that scriptural praise is a multi-faceted activity. Just as we need to broaden our modern understanding of worship to include practical service and inner attitudes, so we need to recognise that praising God involves more than singing loud songs about God.

What does the Hebrew word 'halal' teach you about praise?

....

....

....

What does the Hebrew word 'yadah' teach you about praise?

....

....

....

What does the Hebrew word 'zamar' teach you about praise?

....

....

....

What does the Hebrew word 'shabach' teach you about praise?

....

....

....

What does the Hebrew word 'todah' teach you about praise?

....

....

....

Which of these aspects of praise is least seen in your life and worship? Why is this?

....

....

....

BIBLICAL PRAISE

What do the following passages teach you about praise?

Genesis 1; Job 38:4–7; Psalm 90:14–16; 104:31; Proverbs 8:30–31; Revelation 4:6–11

....

....

Romans 1:21; Ephesians 1:3–14; Philippians 1:11; 1 Peter 2:9; Revelation 16:9

....

....

Psalm 96:11–13; Isaiah 9:2; Luke 2:13–14; Revelation 5:9–14

....

....

Leviticus 23:40; Numbers 10:10; Deuteronomy 27:7

....

....

Deuteronomy 12:7; 16:11–12; Job 1:21

....

....

Exodus 15:20; 2 Samuel 6:14; Psalm 42:4; 149:3; 150

....

....

Mark 2:12; Luke 18:43; Acts 2:46; 3:8; 11:18; 16:25; Ephesians 1:1–14

....

....

What is God saying to you about the way that you praise him?

....

....

....

worship in the old testament

In the Old Testament, worship is the response of God's people to God's revelation of his nature, and this determines the character of his people's response. All Old Testament worship begins by recognising that *Yahweh* is who he is, and that his people are what they are – that he is holy and they are not. The different aspects of worship celebrate the many ways in which God's sinful people can be made fit to encounter his holy presence and experience his holy self.

PLACES OF WORSHIP

What was the Old Testament tabernacle? What did it look like and what did it contain?

....

....

....

What was the purpose of the tabernacle? What did it reveal about God?

....

....

....

Why did God oppose the local sanctuaries?

....

....

Why were some of the prophets unhappy with the temple?

....

....

....

Why did synagogues develop? How did synagogue worship differ from temple worship?

....

....

....

TYPES OF WORSHIP

What do the following passages teach you about the important aspects of Old Testament worship by the people of God?

Jeremiah 6:20 and Amos 4:4

....

....

Genesis 4:3–5; 8:20; Exodus 10:24–26; Numbers 15:1–31; 28–29;

....

....

1 Chronicles 15:16–24; 16:4–7; Ezra 2:40–42; Psalm 22:3; 63:5;

....

....

2 Samuel 6:5; 1 Chronicles 25:1–5; Psalm 42:4; 43:4; 68:25; 81:1–3; 98:4–6; 150:3–5; Isaiah 30:29

....

....

Psalm 26:6; 149:3 and 150:4. 2 Samuel 6:1–22

....

....

Psalms 26:6; 42:4; 48:12–14; 68:24–27 and 118:19

....

....

Psalms 26:6; 46:8–10; 48:8 and 66:5

....

....

Deuteronomy 26:5–10; 1 Samuel 1:1–18, 26; 1 Kings 8: 22–61; 18:36–37; Psalm 5:7; 51:17; 63:4; Isaiah 1:15

....

....

Which aspect of Old Testament worship features most prominently in your worship today? And which features least prominently? Why is this?

....

....

....

....

TIMES FOR WORSHIP

Old Testament worship involved the way that the people lived as well as what they did at the holy places. As God was available to his people at every time and in every place, the local sanctuaries, temple and tabernacle were always open for worship. There were, however, regular special times when all God's people stopped work to join together and celebrate God's grace and goodness.

What is 'the Sabbath' principle? Where does it come from?

....

....

How did God's people use the Sabbath?

....

....

....

What was the purpose of the Passover festival? Where was it celebrated?

....

....

How did God's people use the three annual harvest festivals in worship?

....

....

What was the most important annual festival? Why was it so special?

....

....

....

PROPHETS, PRIESTS AND KINGS

The Old Testament system of formal worship needed some full-time officials to look after the places of worship and supervise what went on. The Scriptures often refer to gatekeepers, musicians and other skilled workers; but the kings, priests and prophets were the key figures.

What was the kings' role in public worship?

....

....

What do these passages reveal to you about the priestly role in worship?

Judges 17:1–13; 1 Samuel 1 – 3:21; Amos 7:10–13

....

1 Samuel 9:3–16

....

Leviticus 10:8–11; 13:1–8; Ezekiel 22:26; 44:23; Haggai 2:11–14

....

Leviticus 1:1–7:38; Numbers 15:1–31 and 28:1–29:40

....

Joshua 3:6–17; 4:9–11

....

Numbers 6:22–26; 1 Samuel 1:17

....

What was the priests' most important function? How did they accomplish this?

....

....

....

What was the prophets' role in worship?

....

....

....

worship in the psalms

How do you use the Psalms in your private worship and devotions?

....
....
....

How does your church use the Psalms in its public worship?

....
....
....

Where do the different Psalms come from?

....
....
....

What can you learn from the titles of the Psalms?

....
....
....

What is king David's relationship with the book of Psalms?

....
....
....

Which is your 'favourite' Psalm? Why is this?

....
....
....
....

TYPES OF PSALMS

The Psalms express the whole range of our human feelings and experiences, from deep depression to ecstatic joy. Some Psalms are wonderful hymns of praise to God, and can be used by worshippers who are at peace with God and the world; other Psalms, however, reflect the dark and painful moments of human experience. Some are for worshippers who recognise that their personal guilt is the cause of their problem; while others are for worshippers who think that they are innocent and should not be suffering at all.

The following Psalms are straightforward hymns of praise. How do they differ from the songs you sing today?

8, 19, 29, 33, 46, 76, 84, 87, 93, 96, 103, 113, 117, 122, 135

....

....

....

....

The following Psalms are laments which address God directly, describe the worshippers misfortunes, and appeal for God's help. How do they differ from the songs you sing today?

3, 4, 5, 7, 12, 16, 26, 31, 38, 44, 51, 55, 60, 63, 74, 79, 86, 102, 121, 125, 130, 137, 143

....

....

....

....

....

The following Psalms are thanksgivings. How do they differ from the songs you sing today?

18, 21, 30, 33, 34, 40, 65, 66, 67, 68, 92, 116, 118, 124, 129, 138, 144

....

....

....

....

....

PROPHETIC PSALMS

Why can we say that Psalms 2, 50, 75, 81–82, 85, 95 and 110 are prophetic? Where may they have come from?

....

....

....

In what way are the following Psalms prophetic? 18, 20, 21, 28, 45, 61, 63, 72, 101, 132, 144

....

....

....

....

Read the following sets of verses. How does each extract from a Psalm point to Jesus?

Psalm 2:7–Acts 13:33 ....

Psalm 8:6–Hebrews 2:6–10 ....

Psalm 16:10–Acts 2:27; 13:35 ....

Psalm 22:8–Matthew 27:43 ....

Psalm 22:16–John 20:25 ....

Psalm 22:18–Mark 15:24 ....

Psalm 40:7–8–Hebrews 10:7 ....

Psalm 41:9–John 13:18 ....

Psalm 45:6–Hebrews 1:8 ....

Psalm 69:9–John 2:17 ....

Psalm 69:21–Matthew 27:34, 48 ....

Psalm 110:4–Hebrews 7:17 ....

Psalm 118:22–Matthew 21:42 ....

Psalm 118:26–Matthew 21:9 ....

Read Psalm 139; what do you think about the following verses?

1–18 ....

....

19–22 ....

....

23–24 ....

....

Why do some believers have difficulties with a few parts of the Psalms?

....

....

....

Suggest three different ways that we could handle these difficult sections?

....

....

....

How did Old Testament Jews use the book of Psalms?

....

....

How did Jesus and the disciples use the book of Psalms?

....

....

How can you use the different types of Psalms to enhance your private and public worship?

....

....

....

....

....

....

worship in the new testament

What do these passages teach you about worship in the New Testament?

....

....

Matthew 4:23:9:35: Mark 1:21

....

....

Luke 1:5–1; 2:22–38; 4:1–38, 44; 6:6; 13:10; 20:1; 24:5–53

....

....

John 2:13–16; 5:1; 6:1–5; 7:1–3; 10:22–30; 13:1

....

....

Acts 2:42–27; 3:1, 8; 5:12, 21

....

....

What two facets of worship were central to the first believers?

....

....

How central are these facets of worship to your life?

....

....

Why did the early church break away from official Judaism?

....

....

....

WORSHIP IN THE EARLY CHURCH

What special services did the early church hold?

....

....

What were the basic ingredients of an early church service?

....

....

....

....

What part did singing play in the early church's worship? What is the New Testament evidence for different types of singing?

....

....

....

What were the different elements of the ministry of the Word in the church's worship? What is the biblical evidence for these elements?

....

....

....

....

....

....

What elements of prayer were used in worship? What is the biblical evidence for these?

....

....

....

....

....

FREEDOM IN WORSHIP

1 Corinthians contains the New Testament's most thorough teaching about worship. In 1 Corinthians 11:2–14:40, Paul deals with the issues which had arisen. It seems that the believers in Corinth had been trying to put Paul's teaching into practice, but that practical difficulties had arisen over freedom and worship, morals and worship, and spiritual gifts and worship.

According to Paul, who could play a full part in every aspect of ministry and worship?

....

....

What was the problem with the women's behaviour?

....

....

....

How was this similar to the problem with meat bought in pagan temples?

....

....

....

What was Paul's solution to the problem with the women's behaviour?

....

....

....

What problems has your church faced in this area? How could Paul's solution be applied to this situation?

....

....

....

What was the problem at the Lord's Supper?

....

....

What was Paul's solution to this problem?

....

....

....

What could your church learn from Paul's teaching about the Lord's Supper?

....

....

....

....

What were the Corinthians' problems with spiritual gifts in worship?

....

....

....

How did Paul deal with these difficulties?

....

....

....

....

What could your church learn from Paul's teaching about spiritual gifts?

....

....

....

....

How does the New Testament re-interpret the Old Testament idea that true worship always involves sacrifice?

....

....

....

....

service and worship

How does the Bible distinguish between spiritual worship and practical service?

....

....

What do Luke 9:46 and John 13:2 suggest to you about the apostles' attitudes to themselves and each other?

....

....

....

....

In what situations do you strive to be the greatest – or not to be the least? Why is this?

....

....

....

What does Jesus' action with the towel teach you about:

greatness ....

....

service ....

....

God ....

....

leadership ....

....

To what sort of serving actions is God calling you?

....

....

....

SELF-RIGHTEOUS SERVICE

If you are to understand and practice 'service in spirit and truth', you must distinguish it from 'self-righteous service'.

If self-righteous service comes through human effort, how does true service come about?

....

....

....

If self-righteous service hopes to be noticed and rewarded, and is impressed by great acts of service, what does true service seek and value?

....

....

....

If self-righteous service is concerned with results and who is served, and is affected by feelings and desires, what is true service concerned with and whom does it serve?

....

....

....

If self-righteous service is a form of self-gratification and self-glorification which damages the community, what is true service and how does it affect the community?

....

....

....

How, specifically, have you served self-righteously? What changes do you need to make to start serving more 'in spirit and truth'?

....

....

....

....

EXPRESSIONS OF SERVICE

Just as we can be tempted to understand worship in terms of 'what we do in church on Sunday', so it can be easy to think of service simply as a list of things that we could or should do. But just as our worship is more than our singing, praying and listening, so our service is more than our cleaning, caring and cooking – it is a continuous way of living rather than a code of ethics or a list of deeds. We should never forget that it is one thing to act like a servant when we feel like it, but quite another thing to be a servant all the time.

How did Tychicus serve? How important would he have seemed at the time?

....

....

....

How did Dorcas serve? How important would she have seemed at the time?

....

....

....

How would other people say that you serve?

....

....

....

....

Why did Peter not want to be served by Jesus?

....

....

....

When have you not wanted to be served? Why is this?

....

....

....

What are the biblical principles of hospitality?

....

....

....

Why is hospitality stressed so strongly in the New Testament?

....

....

....

How do you practise hospitality?

....

....

....

In the last three months, how – practically – have you served?

....

....

....

....

WORSHIP, SERVICE AND HUMILITY

Worship/service is an essentially humble activity. *Shachah* and *proskuneo* – bowing down – are basic biblical words for worship/service, so God's worshippers/servants must have an attitude of humility, of bowing before him, if they are to offer him the worship/service that he both expects and deserves.

How, practically, can you develop humility in your life?

....

....

....

....

giving and worship

Why should we respond to God with giving?

....

....

....

What shows that God is a holy giver?

....

....

....

In the Old Testament, what are the three main forms of giving that the people of Israel use to respond to God's generosity?

....

....

....

When did God's Old Testament people worship him with sacrifices?

....

....

....

What was a tithe?

....

....

To whom did the tithes belong?

....

....

What were tithes used for?

....

....

What was a freewill offering?

....

....

....

For what different purposes were these freewill offerings used?

....

....

....

GIVING AND JESUS

What do these passages teach you about Jesus' attitude to money and giving?

Mark 21:41 ....

....

Matthew 6:24 ....

....

Matthew 19:23–26; Luke 5:1–11, 27–28; 12:33–34; 18:18–23 ....

....

Matthew 25:31–46 ....

....

Luke 10:29–37; 11:42 ....

....

Matthew 5:42; Luke 6:30–38 ....

....

Matthew 6:1–3 ....

....

Luke 14:12–14 ....

....

What do the gifts of the boy in John 6:9 and the widow in Luke 21:1–4 teach you about giving?

....

....

....

How should the principle behind these stories affect your church's attitude to giving and givers?

....

....

....

GIVING AND THE EARLY CHURCH

Why can we say that gifts and giving lead to church growth?

....

....

....

What was special about the giving of the early church in Acts 2:42–47; 3:1–9; 4:32–35?

....

....

....

What is special about the giving in your local church?

....

....

....

Why were Ananias and Sapphira judged so severely?

....

....

....

What does this incident teach you about giving?

....

....

....

What are Paul's three great reasons for giving?

....

....

....

Why do you give?

....

....

....

To whom do you give – and why?

....

....

....

How do you decide how much to give?

....

....

....

Why were Gentile believers instructed that they need not tithe according to the Law of Moses?

....

....

....

What does God expect you to do with your money?

....

....

....

rejoicing and worship

Why can we say that rejoicing, that joy, is at the heart of God's eternal existence?

....

....

....

....

What does this mean for us?

....

....

....

When do we see this divine rejoicing in Jesus' life and ministry?

....

....

....

....

What was the Old Testament year of Jubilee?

....

....

....

What spiritual attitude enabled the people of Israel to keep the provisions of the Jubilee?

....

....

How did Jesus fulfil the Jubilee?

....

....

....

What, practically, can your church learn from the principles of the Jubilee?

....

....

....

BIBLICAL JOY

What do these passages teach you about joy?

Psalm 61:11; Romans 15:13; Philippians 4:4; 1 Peter 1:8; Revelation 19:7 ....

....

....

Philippians 2:2; 1 Thessalonians 2:19–20 ....

....

....

2 Corinthians 6:10; Colossians 1:24 ....

....

....

Philippians 3:1; 4:4; 1 Thessalonians 5:16 ....

....

....

Galatians 5:22 ....

....

What is the relationship between grace and joy?

....

....

....

....

....

What part does joy play in your life?

....

....

....

In the last three months, what has caused you to rejoice?

....

....

....

....

THE SACRIFICE OF PRAISE

What, practically, can you do to develop joy in your life?

....

....

....

....

What does Philippians 4:4–20 teach you about rejoicing?

....

....

....

....

....

....

How does this relate to the Old Testament year of jubilee?

....

....

....

EXPRESSIONS OF REJOICING

What difference does praise and rejoicing make to a local church?

....

....

....

....

....

List all the different ways that you have expressed your praise in the last few months.

....

....

....

....

....

....

....

....

How, practically, could your church provide better opportunities for festivity, celebration and rejoicing?

....

....

....

....

....

....

....

What is the most important truth that you have learnt about rejoicing?

....

....

....

the holy spirit and worship

Worship is the supreme, all-embracing call of the whole Christian church. Before everything else, every expression of the church is called to be a worshipping community. If worship in spirit and truth is not central to every congregation, all other activities must be out of line.

Philippians 3:31 teaches that we worship God 'by the Spirit of God', and this shows that true worship depends entirely on the Holy Spirit. Without his help, we cannot offer one acceptable word or deed of worship to the Father. It is he who inspires our praise and prayers, leads us into the truth, convicts us of our sin, and gives us gifts to help us worship/serve God.

What are the two aspects of Spirit-inspired worship? Why is it important to keep these together?

....
....
....
....

What does Psalm 133 teach you about the Spirit's role in worship/service and unity?

....
....
....
....

What does Ephesians 4:1–16 teach you about the Spirit's role in worship/service and unity?

....
....
....
....

What does Acts 13:1–2 teach you about worship and unity?

....
....
....

To what extent do your church leaders demonstrate the unity seen in the Antioch church?

....

....

....

What does the apostle Paul teach about unity in these passages?

1 Corinthians 1:13 ....

1 Corinthians 3:16 ....

1 Corinthians 3:17 ....

What is the relationship between unity and fellowship?

....

....

How did the believers' expression of fellowship in Acts 2:42–47; 4:32–37 and 1:27–30 affect their worship and the church?

....

....

....

....

How does your church express fellowship? How does this affect the worship and condition of the church?

....

....

....

....

What practical steps can you take to develop unity and to build up your local church?

....

....

....

....

....

THE SPIRIT ENABLES WORSHIP

The book of Acts shows that the Holy Spirit led the first believers to a tremendous depth of worship. What did he inspire and enable them to do?

....

....

....

What does Acts 4:23–31 teach you about the Spirit and worship?

....

....

....

What does Acts 13:1–3 teach you about the Spirit and worship?

....

....

....

Why should the Scriptures be central to worship?

....

....

....

On average, how much time do you give to the Scriptures each day?

....

How important and relevant is the public reading of the Scriptures in church services?

....

....

....

THE SPIRIT BUILDS UP THE CHURCH

What mistakes were the Corinthians making?

....

....

....

What mistakes are your church making?

....

....

....

What are the crucial marks of the Spirit's presence in worship?

....

....

How does Paul encourage believers who feel that they are inferior?

....

....

....

How does he encourage those who think that they are superior?

....

....

....

How would Paul encourage you?

....

....

....

What aspects of your life and service most need to be changed by the 'agape' love of God?

....

....

HEAVENLY WORSHIP

What do these passages teach you about heavenly worship?

Isaiah 6:1–3 ....

Ezekiel 40–47 ....

Luke 2:13–14 ....

Luke 15:7, 10 ....

Revelation 5:11–13; 7:9–10 ....

....

What does the book of Revelation suggest are the two main themes of heavenly worship?

....

....

Which of these two themes is least emphasised in your church's worship? Why is this?

....

....

....

What is the great goal of worship?

....

....

....

What is the most important truth about worship/service that you have learnt in this study?

....

....

....

What is God prompting you to do?

....

....

....

....